One Day At A Time:
Self Healing Journey For The Rejected Soul

Written by: Amber Nicole Bryant
Edited by: Black Eden Publications
Cover & Designed by: Black Eden Publications
Interior Format & Layout: Amber Nicole Bryant
Published: Amber Nicole Bryant

All rights reserved. No part of this publication may be reproduced, stored in a retrial system, distributed, or transmitted in any form or by any means, including photocopying, recording, or other electric, or mechanical methods, without the prior written permission of the author, except in the case of brief quotations with proper reference, embodied in critical reviews and other noncommercial uses permitted by copyright law. For permission requests, write to the author, addressed "Attention: Permissions Coordinator," at the email address below.

Email requests: info@ambernicolebryant.com

Disclaimer

While the author believes that the information and guidance in this book are correct, all parties must rely upon their own skills and judgement when making use of it. The author and/or publisher shall have neither liability nor responsibility to anyone with respect to loss of damaged caused by, or alleged to be caused, directly or indirectly by the information contained in this book.

Copyright © 2020 Amber Nicole Bryant

ISBN 13: 978-0-578-73562-7

Printed in U.S.A

First Printing, 2020

Our work is learning to not to personalize another's refusal to choose us.
- Silvy Khoucasian

Dedication

This book is dedicated to my Abba Father. Thank You Lord for Your unconditional love and grace throughout my self-healing journey. Now, I know that my identity is rooted in who You say I am. I am chosen, set apart, and loved by You, always!

Table of Contents

Introduction	1
Commitment Affirmation	8
Hurts Like Hell	9
Let Me Cry	26
Mad As Hell	42
Why Me	59
Maybe, Maybe Not	74
Choosing To Forgive You	92
It What It Is	108
Give Me Time	125
Re-writing A New Story	141
Scriptures To Remember	155
About The Author	156
Additional Inspiration	157

Introduction

"And then, after your brief suffering, the God of all loving grace, who has called you to share in his eternal glory in Christ, will personally and powerfully restore you and make you stronger than ever.
Yes, he will set you firmly in place and build you up."
-1 Peter 5:10

Introduction

Rejection is inevitable. Everyone who has ever lived, is living, and will live will eventually face rejection. Rejection is the most common emotional wound that all humans sustain at some point in their lives. Whether in relationships, in employment, in business dealings, or at school, expect to be rejected. With the rise and popularity of social media apps such as Facebook, Instagram, Twitter, LinkedIn, and YouTube, we now have to anticipate virtual rejection.

Every once in a while, someone is going to reject one of our friend requests, not like one of our posts, or even delete or block us from their page. While we can quickly recover and heal from an unaccepted friend request or unliked post, nothing, mentally or emotionally, can prepare us for the pain of a spouse leaving, getting fired or laid off from a job, or being ostracized by our friends and family. Those types of rejections crush your soul and can take years to heal from. How do I know this?

I know this because I have faced those types of rejections more times than I would like to count. I know the devastating feeling of a lover unexpectedly breaking up with you or a close friend ending a relationship with you without rhyme or reason.

I have questioned my self-worth, value, and sanity after the person I thought I was going to spend the rest of my life with chose to marry someone else. No emotional feeling has ever rattled the core of my soul like rejection has. The feeling of not being chosen or wanted, ignored, and overlooked hurts like hell.

Introduction

In the immediate aftermath of being rejected by the person we loved or the object of our desire, we feel like the pain of rejection is unbearable. Feelings of hopelessness overwhelms us and makes us believe that we cannot live our lives without the one who has rejected us.

I have spent many sleepless nights crying over lost lovers who rejected me. In those moments of great despair, I understood Toni Braxton's sentiments when she sang "Unbreak My Heart". Her hit song used to be my anthem during those times of heartbreak because I genuinely believed that until they came back to me, I could not move on with my life.

For years, I allowed the residue of past rejections to paralyze me. I lived in constant pain and heartache every day. All I did was go to work, school, and church. I avoided going to social gatherings, dating, and making new friends.

I did everything I could to prevent myself from being emotionally vulnerable with others. I was emotionally and mentally stuck in my own self-imprisonment. Until one day, I decided to take back control of my life. Instead of just merely existing, I wanted to live again. I wanted to heal and be free from the crippling effects of rejection.

In 2016, I began my self-healing journey. I realized that if I wanted to truly heal and be free from the crippling effects of rejection, I had to do the inner work in my heart, mind, and soul. So, I began the process of peeling back the layers of my pain. I spent countless hours sitting in silence asking myself some very difficult questions.

Introduction

As I did my inward soul searching, I unraveled layers of unexpressed and unhealed heartache, resentment, bitterness, unforgiveness, jealously, and insecurity.

All of those buried emotions had to be brought to the surface. In the words of inspirational author, spiritual teacher, life coach, and TV host, Iyanla Vanzant, I had to "call a thing a thing" and acknowledge my unspoken pain, so I could deal with it and let it go.

To assist myself during this journey, I bought several self-help and healing books and watched every Iyanla Vanzant video I could find on YouTube. To this day, I credit her book The Value in the Valley: A Black Woman's Guide through Life's Dilemmas as the game changer in my healing process.

I even took classes from renowned author and spiritual leader, Shannon Evette, on the power of wholeness and healing from past emotional trauma. Those two women were instrumental in giving me the tools I needed to begin and continue along my healing journey.

Healing from past emotional trauma is not easy, and it definitely ain't pretty. Don't get up caught up in believing the lies of the Instagram self-healing gurus who declare that self-love and self-compassion are the only two things you need in your healing process.

To heal from the stronghold of rejection in my life, I had to go through a series of different emotional phases that were triggering and intense. I relied heavily on God's grace and love to push myself through each phase of the process.

Introduction

Through the support of my closest friends, daily prayer, self-reflective journaling, and breakthrough sessions with my Christian counselor, I overcame rejection's bitter sting. In the words of Iyanla Vanzant, "I did the work!" And so, can you!

Do you want to heal from rejection? Are you tired of just existing and going through life's motions? If you are ready to do the work, this book is for you.

To provide you with a road map for recovery, I created this book. During my personal healing journey, I discovered that I had to go through nine different emotional phases to completely heal and be free from rejection. This book is going to take you through each of those nine phases in a unique way.

In each phase, I share a personal story, a phase overview, a four-part self-coaching questionnaire, and a personalized prayer. Each phase will also include some of my personal poems interwoven between each section.

As you go through each of the nine phases, I want you to keep in mind that healing is not linear, and you can experience multiple phases simultaneously. It takes time and a lot of emotional resilience to work through rejection.

Be prepared to experience a wide range of emotions such as denial, sadness, anger, bitterness, and unforgiveness, but give yourself time and grace to work through them. I am a living testimony that you can heal from rejection if you commit to doing the daily inner work.

Introduction

Rejection does not have to define you unless you allow it to. Learn from me and don't allow the feelings of rejection to consume you and waste precious years of your life. Take this time and heal the broken pieces of your fragmented soul.

Everything you need to go through this journey, you already possess inside of you. Just be patient with yourself. And, on the days that you want to give up and throw in the towel, remember I am rooting and praying for you.

Introduction

Today Is The Day

Today is the day I live and not die.
Today is the day I get up and try.
Today is the day I leave my past behind.
Today is the day I renew my mind.
Today is the day I walk in my calling.
Today is the day I quit stalling.
Today is the day I pass the test.
Today is the day I give it my best.
Today is the day that I let go of everyone and everything holding me back.
Today is the day I get my life back on track.
Today is the day I allow myself to heal and be free.
Today is the day I forgive those who have hurt me.
Today is the day I let go of fear.
Today is the day I cry my last tear.
Today is the day I cross the finish line.
Today is the day I seek after what is mine.
Today is the day I do what is right.
Today is the day I live by faith and not by sight.
Today is the day I make better choices.
Today is the day I become one of the voices.
Today is the day I encourage myself.
Today is the day I help someone else.
Today is the day that I will win.
Today is the day my healing journey begins.

Introduction

Prayer

Dear Heavenly Father,

I honor You. I bless Your Holy name. You are the Most High God and You are worthy to be praised.

Today as I approach Your throne of grace in my time of need, I pray that You hear and grant the petitions of my heart.

Father, I know You are the Healer of the brokenhearted and near to those who are crushed in their spirit (Psalm 34:18). The wounds of rejection have pierced my soul. The pain of not being chosen and wanted by those I have loved feels unbearable, but I know through Your love, power, and strength I can endure all things.

As I go through this journey of healing, I ask that You grant me wisdom, knowledge, and understanding on how to navigate through my feelings and make peace with my past.

I ask all these things in Your Son Jesus name. Amen

Commitment Page

I promise to make time everyday to read, reflect, and do the written Self-Coaching questions at the end of each phase.

I am committed to doing the daily inner work to heal my mind, heart, soul, and spirit from the shackles of rejection.

No matter how hard it gets or how emotional I feel, I will not quit this journey. I will pray and get through this journey one day at a time.

_____

Signature

_____

Date

Hurts Like Hell

"The truth will set you free."
-John 8:32

Revolving Doors

I experienced the biggest breakthrough in my healing journey when I acknowledged my feelings about my father's rejection of me. Before I came out of my mother's womb, my biological father told my mother that I was not his child. This left my mother heartbroken, and the seeds of her pain grew inside of me.

During my childhood years, I despised my father. I would always remind my mother that he rejected and abandoned her during her pregnancy, but not only did he reject her, he rejected me too, and I resented him for that.

I hated my father as a teenager. No matter what he did, the $50 birthday cards, unexpected visits, or small tokens of affection he gave me never erased the fact that he was a deadbeat and an absentee father. My father rejected me then, and he still rejects me to this day. And that rejection has carried over into my romantic relationships.

Every man I have ever truly loved has rejected me. Like a revolving door, they would come in and out of my life, like my father did. One minute, they would confess their undying love for me, and then the next minute, they would disappear from my life without a trace. Then, as soon as I got the strength and courage to let them go, they would unexpectedly pop back up in my life and ask me for another chance.

Because I was so broken, so desperate for a crumb of love, I would take them back. This repetitive, toxic cycle went on for years until I watched a YouTube video of Iyanla Vanzant tell a young woman who appeared to be my age, in her early 30s, that the root of her bad relationship patterns with men was her unacknowledged and unhealed pain of her father's rejection of her.

Hurts Like Hell

My God! It was like Iyanla was looking into the camera and speaking directly to me. As the young woman accepted her pronouncement and cried on Iyanla's shoulder, I cried with her.

As the tears streamed from my eyes, and my sobs grew louder and uglier, I realized that the men I dated in my past were reflections of my father. Subconsciously, I chose men who embodied the characteristics of him. Like my father, they would show up in my life, woo me, disappear, and then come back again.

No matter how many times they cheated on me, lied to me, disrespected me, or made a complete fool of me, I always gave them another chance, just like I gave my father.

My ex-boyfriends and past lovers were mirrors of my father. The love and acceptance I thought I was seeking from them was the love and acceptance I really wanted from my father. After my song and dance with each of them ended, I pretended to my family and friends that I was unfazed. I proudly boasted to them that I was good and that the men would be back.

I even tried to make myself believe that I was unbothered by their inability to love and choose me. The keyword is tried. On the outside, I had this superpower of acting like I was strong as steel, but on the inside, my heart was drowning in sorrow. I wanted them to love me, to choose me, to miss me, to need me, to want me. I felt validated when they came back, but they never came back because they loved me, only because I kept the door open...the same door I held open for my father.

Hurts Like Hell

It took me years, 30 in fact, to admit that the revolving door of my past relationships were opened by my father. But, if I wanted to close the door, stop the cycles, and heal the pain, I had to acknowledge that my father's rejection of me hurts like hell.

Hurts Like Hell

Heartless

I want to become heartless; I want my heart to be empty.
I want it to be emotionless. I don't want it to feel love, passion, sadness, anger, or even sympathy.
I don't want to fall in love anymore; I just want to be free—free from hurt, lies, pain, heartbreak, and misery.
I want to be heartless, and if I could, I would.
To be heartless, you can't have a heart, and I do.
So, I guess I will have to feel these emotions and somehow make it through.

Hurts Like Hell

Your heart has been shattered into a million pieces. Your stomach is in knots, and the wind has been knocked out of your lungs. Tears stream down your eyes like waterfalls. The pain is intense. You feel like you're dying. You want to scream, but your mouth fails to make a sound. You want to run away, but where will you go? So, you just stand there heartbroken, disappointed, shocked, enraged...rejected. No emotional wound cuts deep into the soul like rejection does.

The initial feeling you experience when it occurs makes you wish you were never born. The extremeness of the pain feels unbearable. Every time one of my past lovers rejected me, that is how I felt. Yet, I masked my hurt. I pretended it didn't bother me. I even tried to convince myself that I didn't care, but I did. I became skilled at repressing, denying, and rejecting my emotions. Avoidance seemed like a healthy coping mechanism for the continuous rejection I faced, but the more I denied my feelings, the more I suffered.

I have learned that not feeling your feelings doesn't make them go away, and leaving words unspoken doesn't mean they don't need to be expressed and addressed. Just because you don't acknowledge your pain doesn't mean that it doesn't exist. In order to heal from rejection, you have to acknowledge and experience the pain and heartache. Ignoring and denying how you feel immediately after you face rejection only prolongs your suffering and delays your healing. Allow yourself time to process your hurt feelings.

Hurts Like Hell

Putting on a brave face and trying to make yourself and others believe that you're "good" and "okay" when you're really not is the worst thing you can do for your mental, emotional, spiritual, and even physical health. I have suffered many sicknesses from the root of a broken heart, so don't repress your feelings no matter how bad they make you feel or bruise your ego.

Being able to feel your feelings is a hard and courageous thing to do. When we avoid and numb our pain, our pain only increases. It took courage for me to admit to myself and others that I wasn't okay. Today, I want you to make a conscious effort to run towards your emotions, rather than away from them.

Feel what you need to feel and then let it go. Give yourself permission to be vulnerable and experience the fleeting emotions of disbelief, hurt, anger, frustration, and disappointment. Acknowledge your pain. Give it a voice. Give it a sound. Cry if you need to cry and scream if you need to scream. Write if you need to write. Allow everything that is buried deep within you to come up to the surface. Trust yourself and trust God that He will give you the grace and strength to survive and endure the gravity of your emotions.

As you go through this phase of healing, I want you to become aware of patterns like detaching, masking, and distracting yourself whenever you begin to feel the intensity of the feelings of rejection. When these emotions arise, surrender to them and remove all judgments, conditions, and time limits on why you feel them or how long you will experience them.

Hurts Like Hell

Acknowledge them, feel them, and then release them. The easiest way out of anything is through. Sometimes, allowing yourself to feel your feelings reduces their intensity and makes them go away quicker.

Get in the habit of consistently sitting with your feelings, even the uncomfortable and uneasy ones. Be present in those moments. Listen to what your inner thoughts are saying and how your body feels. It's time. The rejection happened, and it crushed your soul.

Hurts Like Hell

Rejected

I feel rejected...used.
Unwanted...confused.
I can't begin to analyze or even try to rationalize why or how you could treat me this way.
It's even more painful how you won't even respond to me and just go on living day-to-day.
Are you that heartless that you feel no empathy?
At least, you could show me a little compassion and have a little sympathy.
But the seconds turn into minutes, and the minutes turn into hours, and the hours turn into days...and finally the days have turned into weeks, and you still haven't bothered to call.
Now, I have to simply face the fact that you never cared at all.

━━ **Hurts Like Hell** ━━

Circumstance Questions

What type of rejection did you experience?
_____
_____
_____

When did you experience the rejection?
_____
_____
_____

Describe in detail how the rejection happened?
_____
_____
_____
_____
_____
_____

What did you do as a result of this rejection? ex. Cry, break something, self - harm, harm the people responsible, etc...
_____
_____
_____
_____
_____
_____
_____

Hurts Like Hell
Thought Questions

What is your definition of hurting like hell?

What were the thoughts that were going on in your mind during the rejection?

Do you believe that the rejection was intentional, unintentional, or a misunderstanding?

Hurts Like Hell
Thought Questions

Re-read your version of the story, what thoughts are replaying in your mind? What are you continuously thinking and telling yourself? Please list them out.

What is your most hurtful thought concerning the rejection?

Are your thoughts true? What evidence do you have to support for or against them?

Hurts Like Hell

Thought Questions

Are you avoiding dealing with your rejection? Have you developed one of these negative defense mechanisms to help you cope? Give an example if you have used one of the listed mechanisms.

Compensation | **Example**

Counterbalancing the pain of your rejection by involving yourself in a good cause or project to avoid dealing with the pain.

Denial | **Example**

The refusal to accept the reality of your rejection. Acting as if the rejection never happened.

Rationalization | **Example**

Trying try to explain or justify the reason why you were rejected in a way that lessens the pain and makes it easier for you to accept.

Hurts Like Hell

Repression

Unconsciously blocking your thoughts, feelings, and impulses about the rejection. Not talking about it with others or finding ways not to think about it.

Example

Projection

Projecting your thoughts, feelings, and impulses about the rejection onto the other people.

Example

Displacement

Transferring your emotions about the person that rejected you onto other people. Lashing out your sadness or frustration on others.

Example

Avoidance

Avoiding taking about the rejection and how you feel about it. Avoiding people, places, and things that remind of you the person that rejected you.

Example

— Hurts Like Hell —

Feeling Questions

Identify Your Emotions

Circle all of the emotions you have felt since the rejection.

angry	hurt	frustrated	enraged	sad
useless	confused	miserable	disappointed	
hopeless	abandoned	belittled	betrayed	
overwhelmed	neglected	depressed	ignored	
manipulated	shamed	dismissed		

When you feel rejected, what parts of your body do you feel the pain in?

_____
_____
_____

If your feelings could speak what would they say...

_____
_____
_____
_____
_____
_____

═══Hurts Like Hell═══

Action Questions

What Unexpressed Pain Looks Like

How is your rejection being projected in your daily life? (check boxes)

☐ **Numbing yourself and hiding your real feelings**

☐ **Perfectionism and overachieving**

☐ **Constantly staying busying with projects or work**

☐ **Engaging in reckless behavior (sex, drugs, or alcohol)**

After identifying the negative coping mechanisms you have been using, release the negative behaviors attached to them and replace them with positive ones.

I release these negative behaviors:

_____
_____
_____
_____

I replace them with these positive behaviors:

_____
_____
_____
_____

Hurts Like Hell

Action Questions

Write a letter to the person who rejected you. Truly acknowledge how you feel. Release everything that is stored in your heart.

_____
_____
_____
_____
_____
_____
_____
_____
_____
_____
_____
_____
_____
_____
_____
_____
_____
_____
_____
_____
_____
_____

Hurts Like Hell

Prayer

Dear Heavenly Father,

You are a great an awesome God and I give You the praise, honor, and glory due to Your name.

Father, I am experiencing deep emotional anguish in my heart and soul as a result of the rejection I have faced. Holy Spirit reveal to me the emotions that I am harboring deep within my soul that I need to work through and release. Father, give me the grace to unpack all of my unexpressed pain, anger, sadness, and shame.

Infuse me with the fruit of the Holy Spirit, joy, peace, patience, kindness, goodness, faithfulness, gentleness, and self-control (Galatians 5:22-23) as I release bitterness, rage, anger, revenge, profanity, and slander (Ephesians 4:31).

As I process and release these emotions, surround me with Your presence and love. Thank You Father.

I pray this prayer in Your Son Jesus name. Amen

Let Me Cry

"A time to cry."
-Ecclesiastes 3:4

Let Me Cry

The Perfect Nightmare

I started dating my Mr. Perfect in February of 2011, and by the end of April, I was in full-blown love with him. You couldn't tell me nothing about that man. He was my prince charming, and he treated me like a queen! For sure, I thought he was going to be my husband. We talked about marriage all the time.

He was the perfect boyfriend—sweet, romantic, kind, intelligent, and fine! Plus, he always planned all of our dates. All I had to do was dress cute and show up, and he took care of the rest. Our relationship seemed like something out of a fairytale, but he taught me the hard way that fairytales are not real. If it seems too good to be true, usually, it is, and that was the case with him and our relationship. My once seemingly perfect dream quickly turned into a nightmare.

By the end of July, Mr. Perfect turned into Mr. Narcissist. Our relationship was crumbling, and I was holding onto it by a thread. I knew deep down in my heart that the relationship was over, yet I would not let him go. I kept hoping and praying that he would go back to the way he once was—perfect.

My perfect boyfriend became emotionally and mentally abusive. He would disappear for days and then pop back up like nothing happened. In retrospection, he was probably out cheating, but back then, I blamed it on the fact that his son and son's mother was moving out of state. He had a really close relationship with his son, and I thought his erratic behavior and disappearing acts was because of the pain he was feeling of their soon-to-be departure.

Let Me Cry

Perhaps, that played some part in it, but, in reality, he just wanted the relationship to be over and didn't have the courage to break up with me. Years later, he told me that he knew I deserved better because he wasn't a good man. Translation: He was tired of being faithful and being in a committed relationship, and he wanted to get back to his player lifestyle and continue hosting his wild house parties. Oh, that is a story for another day, or perhaps another phase!

His infamous boozed-filled, drug-laced, group sex parties were the talk of the town! Yet, I didn't find out about them until after the relationship was over. To this day, I don't know how I found his secret YouTube page, but I did, and luckily for me, he recorded all the parties and uploaded them onto the page. And, you better believe I watched every last one of them. Talk about a nightmare!

Who the f*ck did I date? Mr. Perfect must've had an evil twin because surely that wasn't the same man I dated, not my prince charming! While I didn't find out about his infamous parties until after the breakup, it was the unraveling of his 10-page criminal rap sheet that finally broke the camel's back.

At this point, I had to face the fact that Mr. Perfect was Mr. Liar! But, even with all this information, I still wouldn't let him go…well, I tried, but when I did, he wouldn't let me. His protests to my attempts to break things off with him gave me false hope that he wanted the relationship to work, but he didn't.

It was just his ego. Eventually, he got tired of playing the cat-and-mouse game with me and we broke up on August 8.

Let Me Cry

I will never forget that day. It was a hot summer day, and the temperature was hell degrees. After not answering my calls that morning, I unexpectedly drove to his house. Like always, his front door was unlocked, and I walked right in and found him lying in a drunken haze on his couch.

Immediately, I began screaming and yelling at him, but he just laid there, numb. Unfazed by my antics, he got up and walked outside. I became even more irritated at this point and began pushing him. Finally, he had enough and knocked on one of his neighbor's door. An older man opened the door and let him inside, and that was the end of our relationship. The fairytale ended at that moment. He didn't have to say that it was over; for me, it was over!

As he walked inside his neighbor's house, and the door slammed shut behind him, my heart broke into a million pieces in his driveway. I stood there in disbelief. He didn't even have the guts to face me. He just ran away like a punk!

But it was over, and it was time for me to leave. Welp, not so fast! Like a scene in a movie, my car wouldn't start. So, I called my best friend, and she and her boyfriend came over and gave me a jump. Later that night, one of my other close friends called me. I had texted her earlier and told her about what had transpired. To my surprise, she wasn't a bit shocked about what happened.

She knew from the beginning that his "Mr. Perfect" act was just a façade. If only I would have listened to her constant warnings about him in the beginning. Nevertheless, she was a great friend through it all. She asked me that night, "What do you need from me during this time?" In a muffled voice, I told her, "Just let me cry."

From Sunup To Sundown

I am here physically, but mentally, I am gone. And emotionally, I am dead.
Laying here, paralyzed in my bed.
Dawn turned into afternoon, and afternoon turned into evening, and evening into night.
Till finally the moon is replaced by the sun's bright light.
Raindrops hit my windowpane.
Yet, the tears that fall from my eyes fall faster than the rain.
My heart aches.
How much more can I take?
I try to fall asleep, but images of you and me play in repeat in my head,
and all I can hear are the last words that you said.
I try to analyze,
rationalize,
but nothing seems to make sense.
Why does this have to be so intense?
And, the cycle starts all over again as I see the rays from the morning sun.
When will this cycle be done?

Let Me Cry

Rejection is God's protection. Rejection is redirection. How many times have you heard those clichés from people after you've been rejected? Yes, in most cases, rejection is God's protection and divine redirection, but in the moment of feeling rejected, you don't want to hear that.

Those sayings, while true, don't take away rejection's sting. They don't make you feel any better. They don't make the person who broke your heart unbreak it or the company that fired you call and give you your job back. Though our friends and family mean well, telling us to "just get over it" doesn't stop our pain or make us heal quicker.

When people tell us to just move on, they are, unintentionally, or perhaps, intentionally, telling us that our feelings don't matter. That is not what we need to hear, because our feelings do matter.

When trying to process and overcome rejection, we need people in our corner who will create and hold spaces for us to feel our feelings and go through the grieving process. Comforting words are nice, and, at times, very much needed, but sometimes, the greatest thing our friends and loved ones can do for us is just let us cry.

Adapting to change and loss takes energy and time. Before you can truly do the inner healing work in your soul, you have to grieve. Grieve the end of the relationship. Grieve the end of the friendship. Grieve the 'no' that you received. Grieve the possibility of what could have been, but never will be. You have to grieve, and grieving is draining and exhausting. When you're going through rejection, pain feels like your enemy, but pain is not your enemy.

Let Me Cry

Pain is an indicator that there is something inside of you that needs to heal. The pain of rejection is overwhelming and devastating, but in order to heal, you have to feel it.

Yes, rejection hurts, but what hurts even worse is ignoring the gaping hole in your heart and not acknowledging its void. Recovering from rejection forces you to be vulnerable and completely honest with yourself about how you feel. It makes you stop pretending that you're fine when you're really not. It is okay not to be okay, and during this phase of the healing process, you are not okay.

So, allow yourself to mourn, to grieve, and to cry. Ignore the people who tell you to just "get over it and move on." Yes, eventually, you will get over it, and you will move on, but right now is not that time. Now is the time to deal with the pain because if you don't, it will keep lingering in your soul until you feel it and heal it.

As you go through this phase, there will be days when your feelings will take you down an emotional rollercoaster. There will be days when all you want to do is cry or other days when you will go through a sequence of different emotions. Just go with the flow. If sadness comes, let it come. If anger rises, let it rise. If you want to sit at home and binge watch Netflix all day, binge watch away.

Allow yourself to be human, even if that means being labeled an emotional mess by others. Don't feel bad or guilty about those days. Feel the emotions and let them go. It is okay to feel hurt. It is okay to cry. Crying is a healthy way to cope with your pain, so let the tears fall and feel the sadness that you have stored within your heart and soul. You will endure the pain with God's help and love.

Let Me Cry

During this time, it is important to not allow others to expect more from you than you feel comfortable giving. There are going to be days when you will not feel like being responsible and present or even getting out of bed. Sometimes, you will cry in front of people and expose your sadness, irritability, and anger. Resist the need to act like you have it all together. You are going to fall apart some days, and that's okay because it is all a part of the process.

While I advocate for falling apart, I do not endorse engaging in unhealthy habits or bad coping mechanisms. In the past, I have used sex as a way to ease my pain from rejection. But sex never eased my pain. While sex may not be your vice, drugs, alcohol, overworking, and overachieving don't work either. Indulging in compulsive and addictive behaviors doesn't make the pain of rejection go away. You can keep yourself busy from sunup to sundown, but when you get home, the pain will be waiting for you at the door. You cannot escape or run away from the pain.

Take responsibility for your feelings and behaviors and find healthy ways to cope and take care of yourself. Don't let your grief and pain control you. Surrendering to the pain is not an excuse to cause additional internal or external pain to yourself and others. One thing I've learned about pain is it isn't a permanent condition, unless you allow it to be.

The pain will stop once you fully embrace it, feel it, and go through it. Don't try to analyze, rationalize, or justify your feelings. Clarity and healing will come later. Trust yourself that you are strong enough to survive the discomfort and temporary feelings of emotional pain. You may hurt for a while, but peace, love, and acceptance are on the other side of the pain.

In Limbo

Doing my best to hold on.
Lord knows I am trying to be strong.
Every day seems cloudy, no glimmer of sunshine; all I see is rain,
and all I feel is pain.
All I want is one last conversation,
just an explanation
of why I'm being left in limbo,
having to pick up the pieces and just go.
What about my feelings? Damn, did you even care?
But like they say...life isn't fair.
So, I'm trying to keep going,
forever not knowing.

Let Me Cry

Circumstance Questions

How long has it been since the rejection has happened?
_____
_____
_____

Has the pain gotten better or worse?
_____
_____

Describe how you are currently coping with the rejection?
_____
_____
_____
_____
_____

Are your current coping strategies getting your closer or further away from healing from the rejection?
_____
_____
_____
_____
_____
_____
_____
_____
_____

Let Me Cry
Thought Questions

Are you preventing yourself from mourning or grieving the rejection? If yes, why?

If no, how you are mourning or grieving it?

How does your rejection affect your day to day lifestyle?

— Let Me Cry —

Thought Questions

To Fully Mourn My Rejection

Finish each statement and answer how you will let go of each.

To fully mourn my rejection, I let go of these thoughts: (ex. can't manage without him/her):

_____
_____
_____
_____
_____

To fully mourn my rejection, I let go of this guilt:

_____
_____
_____
_____
_____

To fully mourn my rejection, I let go of these plans for the future:

_____
_____
_____
_____
_____

To fully mourn my rejection, I let go of these painful memories:

_____
_____
_____
_____
_____

To fully mourn my rejection, I let go of these unspoken words:

_____
_____
_____
_____
_____

To fully mourn my rejection, I let go of these lost opportunities:

_____
_____
_____
_____
_____

===== Let Me Cry =====

Feeling Questions

What are your current feelings about the rejection now? Are they good are bad?

_____
_____
_____
_____
_____

What is your main emotion? (ex. Angry, Sad, Hurt etc.) On a scale of 1-10, what is the intensity of this emotion?

_____
_____
_____
_____
_____
_____
_____

What other feelings or emotions are you experiencing?

_____
_____
_____
_____
_____
_____
_____

Let Me Cry

Action Questions

How Am I Coping?

Which of these responses currently describe how you are currently coping with the rejection? (check box)

- ☐ **Overindulging in food or loss of appetite**

- ☐ **Binging watching Netflix or other movies or TV shows**

- ☐ **Using drugs, alcohol, or sex to numb the pain**

- ☐ **Barely sleeping or not sleeping at all**

- ☐ **Crying constantly**

- ☐ **Social withdrawal and isolation**

- ☐ **Lack of focus at school or at work**

- ☐ **Snapping at others**

- ☐ **Unmotivated to do anything**

- ☐ **Blaming yourself for the rejection**

- ☐ **Talking about the rejection constantly to friends and family**

Let Me Cry

Action Questions

When I Am Sad I Will

Meditate on these scriptures:

Listen to these songs:

Watch these shows or movies:

Call and talk to these people:

Remind myself these things:

Go to these places:

Eat these foods:

Do these self-care rituals:

— Let Me Cry —

Action Questions

List three things you will implement in your daily life to help you heal from the rejection.

1.

2.

3.

Who are three people you can reach out to that will support your feelings and allow you to have a judgement free zone?

1.

2.

3.

Let Me Cry

Prayer

Dear Heavenly Father,

Thank You for Your infinite love and care. I praise You just because of who You are. You are the Kings of Kings, the Lord of Lords, and the Holy One of Israel.

Lord, the sadness of rejection is consuming me. My heart aches every day. Please heal my broken heart and bind up my emotional wounds of rejection. Remove the hurt that I am holding in my heart.

Lord, for my heaviness of heart, give me the garment of praise. For my constant mourning, give me unspeakable joy, and for the pain I have suffered, give me a double portion of happiness and peace.

I ask all these things in Your Son Jesus name. Amen

Mad As Hell

"But don't let the passion of your emotions lead you to sin! Don't let anger control you or be fuel for revenge, not for even a day."
-Ephesians 4:26

Mad As Hell

Two Wrongs Do Not Make A Right

He's married! Not just in a relationship...married!" My heart couldn't take it. I couldn't believe the words coming out of my friend's mouth. I knew he wasn't lying to me, but still, married? Did he just say the man who was just at my house, sitting next to me in my living room was married? Surely, he meant him and ole girl were still dating. Engaged, perhaps, but married?! Naw, that just couldn't be, but it was.

As I processed these thoughts in my head, the anger inside of me began to rise like ashes out of a volcano. After all he and I had been through, he didn't even have the decency or the respect to tell me he was married. He knew damn well that I didn't know. It was only after I rejected his sexual advances towards me that he finally blurted out that "technically," he wasn't "single." I didn't know what "technically not single" meant. We had been talking for over two weeks before he came to my house, so he had ample time to tell me that he was married!

The more I began to think about it, the angrier I became. My friend kept giving me the details about Mr. Married and his new bride as he continued to scroll through their Facebook pages. I guess if I would have looked at his page, I would've known that he was married too, but for the sake of my healing process, in order to get over him, I avoided looking at all of his social media accounts. Hell, I had just unblocked him from my phone a month prior to him contacting me out of the blue.

Mad As Hell

My friend knew my mind was racing, so he snapped me back into reality. "Amber, what are you going to do?" Good question. What was I going to do? At first, I was just going to do what I had always done when I ended things with men—block them and keep it moving. I had learned from the last time I snapped at one of my exes that the possibility of me going to jail was real. Let's just say, I almost got arrested, but luckily, I was friends with the police officer who arrived on the scene…a story for another book.

This time, I was going to bow out gracefully until my friend said, "You should tell his wife." Tell his wife? Was he crazy?! That is crazy. Who has time for that drama?! As he kept making his case on why I should tell her, my mind began to go into a dark place, the place it went to the last time I almost got arrested. A voice in my head said, "Yeah, tell her." I began to wrestle within myself. If I told her, will she believe me? Will she leave him? Will she want to fight me? What will she do? What would I do? Does Jesus want me to do this? It was like my friend and the voice in my head were in cahoots because he answered my last unspoken thought.

"God wants you to tell her, Amber. She deserves to know. Wouldn't you want to know if it was you?" he asked, convincingly. I began to stutter. "Well, well, well, yeah, I guess." "You guess?" he screamed.

The voice in my head echoed his sentiments. I was torn. I said I was just going to let it go, but my friend and the voice in my head were not having it. My friend was in the process of getting divorced himself. Shortly after getting married, he found out that his wife had been having an affair on him. It broke him. It broke me too. He was a great guy and a loyal and loving husband to her.

Mad As Hell

"Amber, you know how I found out, how much it hurt me. Doesn't she deserve to know? They haven't even been married for 90 days yet." My friend had a point.

He convinced me. I had the receipts—all the scandalous texts he had sent me—so I did the unthinkable. I sent his wife a Facebook message and told her everything. Everything? Everything! Initially, she didn't believe me. I knew she wouldn't, but, baby, I had receipts! Once I sent them to her, the conversation took an unexpected turn I was not ready for.

"Okay, since you're telling me this, did he tell you that he has a baby on the way? Did he tell you that I'm pregnant?" she replied in all caps. A baby? Did she say a "baby"? Wait, one minute! Not only did Mr. Married not mention that he was married, but he totally bypassed telling me that he had a baby on the way too! Let's just say, at this point, I became mad as hell, and the voice in my head totally took over my mind and fingers.

I messaged his wife at 11 a.m., and the conversation didn't end until 11 p.m. that night. He even had the audacity to jump in our conversation at one point and tell me that I was lying. Again, I sent those receipts! And, he never responded.

Finally, guilt begin to consume me. It was like the Lord allowed me to feel her pain, and I instantly regretted what I had done. I let my anger get the best of me. Yes, Mr. Married was wrong, dead wrong, but who was I to be the judge and jury and tell his wife? He was wrong, but so was I.

Mad As Hell

Good Gril Gone Bad

I want to cry. I want to scream.
I wish I could just wake up from this and say it was all a dream.
I guess you can say from this day forward, I am a good girl gone bad,
but I ain't the type of girl who just sits back and dwells on what I had.
At the end of the day, you can say I'm still a little bitter and mad.
But it's all good because life is treating me good.
I wouldn't turn back the hands of time if I could.
See, in this life, you gotta play the game, or the game will play you.
But I done played it, got played, and that's just how the game gon' do.
You see, when you play with fire, you better believe you gon' get burned.
But, I'm a soldier, so I dust myself off and take it as a lesson learned.
So sad that it has to be this way.
Call it from now, I really can't say.
All I know is from this day forward, I am a good girl gone bad,
with a real strong vengeance for any man who crosses my path. Damn, that's what happens to a good girl when she gets mad.

Mad As Hell

Anger is a negative emotion. Well, at least, that's what we have been taught. Is anger really a "bad" emotion? I guess if you listen to society it is, but the Bible clearly tells us in Ephesians 4:26, to be "angry, but sin not." Clearly, God doesn't mind if we're angry. Even God gets angry. But feeling angry doesn't give us a license to sin or hurt others.

Anger is a natural human emotion that we all feel when we experience emotional, mental, or physical pain. Anger is a warning signal. It signals when we have been offended, violated, disrespected, or when a problem in our lives arises and needs to be solved. Anger is an internal red flag system that brings us into awareness of something that needs to be addressed.

Normally, we experience anger on two levels. First, we experience the immediate feeling of anger that makes us want to cuss somebody out, scream, yell, and fight. Then, there's the second level of anger: the anger that we hide and repress and let stew deep within our soul. This level of anger is born out of repeated pain. When this type of anger goes unacknowledged and unexpressed, it develops into rage. Unlike anger, rage is a negative, destructive emotion, and when acted upon, it can cause irreparable health conditions and relationship problems.

When you've been rejected it is very important that you manage your anger in a healthy way so it doesn't turn into rage. It is okay to be angry with the person who rejected you. You have a right to be angry. Feeling angry at the person who rejected you is a natural response and is a necessary part of the healing process.

Remember, healing is an emotional rollercoaster and anger is a part of the ride. Acknowledge your anger and allow your feelings to come to the surface. Feel the feelings of anguish, hurt, and pain. Don't deny or repress your anger because anger that festers has the potential to turn into bitterness. And I don't care how strong you consider yourself to be or how solid your spiritual walk with God is, you will feel, at times, an overwhelming temptation to feel bitter or, even worse, want to punish or get even with the person who rejected you.

Those are normal feelings, but don't act on them. As tempting as it may be, resist the urge to seek revenge on the person who rejected you. If someone chooses to walk out of your life or not choose you, that is their right. You have to accept that and eventually be okay with their choice. Actively seeking revenge will not help you heal or move on quicker. Instead, it will block you and keep you stuck in a perpetual cycle of pain. You cannot make someone love you or want to be with you, and as Oprah said it best, "I don't want anyone who doesn't want me."

On the other hand, just like they have the right to reject you, you also have the right to express to them how you feel about it. If you get the opportunity to express your anger to the person who rejected you, please, do it constructively.

Your objective for the conversation should be letting them know how you feel, so you can get the feelings out of your system. It's not about their response. Whether they respond positively or negatively, you said what you had to say and made your peace. You cannot control how they will respond or if they will respond. All you can control is how you respond. And, hopefully, if you learned anything from my personal story, two wrongs do not make a right.

Mad As Hell

Again, it is okay to be angry. Connect with your angry feelings. Own them, feel them, express them, write them down, paint them, and then release them and be done with them. Learn how to cope with your anger in healthy ways, so you can protect yourself from further disappointment and harm. When you process and examine the reasons for your anger, you are better able to understand your triggers and choose better responses. Anger can be a beneficial emotion if you don't allow it to consume you and turn into bitterness. Be angry, but sin not.

Mad As Hell

Still Mad

I used to be so optimistic,
but then, I became another statistic.
So now, I view life a little bit more realistic.
I used to be a hopeless romantic,
but now, the thought of falling in love again
makes me panic— to give my heart away again,
to utter those words, "I have a boyfriend."
I was so in love, so carefree.
Then, you hurt me,
and my whole world changed.
I became hostile, angry, bitter, and even, at times, a bit deranged.
I lost my mind.
I crossed that thin line.
Promises of forever,
we would be together.
But you changed. Your heart turned cold,
and my heart was left on hold.
I planned out our whole life.
I knew without a doubt I was going to be your wife,
but, then, you walked away,
and I haven't gotten over it to this day.

Mad As Hell

Circumstance Questions

Have you expressed your anger to the person that rejected you? If so, describe in detail what you said and did. How did they respond?

_____
_____
_____
_____
_____
_____
_____
_____

Was the outcome what you were hoping or expecting for?

_____
_____
_____

If you expressed your anger towards them negatively, have you apologized to them and explained to them that your behavior was wrong?

_____
_____
_____
_____
_____
_____

Mad As Hell

Thought Questions

How does your anger with the person that rejected you show up in your daily life?

How did your parents or those you grew up around deal with anger when you were growing up?

What do you believe is the "right way" to deal with anger? Is that "way" actually true, good, helpful, healthy, and right?

Mad As Hell
Thought Questions

Do you want to seek revenge on the person that rejected you?

If so, how will that help you in your healing process?

Have you been rejected like this in a similar manner before?

Are you still angry at that person as well?

The last time you withheld your anger it caused a problem by...

The last time you got angry what did you do?

Did your anger get you the results you wanted?

Do you feel like you have anger issues?

Mad As Hell

Feeling Questions

Describe Your Anger

Circle all of the words that describe your anger

---
annoyed   irritated   frustrated   provoked

antagonized   resentful   pissed off   betrayed

disgusted   outraged   furious   enraged

What feelings are underneath your anger? (ex. Grief, confusion, sadness, disbelief etc.)

_____
_____
_____
_____
_____

Do you feel like you have a right to be angry with the person that rejected you? Why?

_____
_____
_____
_____
_____

Mad As Hell

Feeling Questions

What Triggered Me

Check all the statements that caused you to feel triggered.

- [ ] I felt powerless
- [ ] I felt blamed
- [ ] I felt frustrated
- [ ] I felt unheard
- [ ] I felt lied to
- [ ] I felt disrespected
- [ ] I felt manipulated
- [ ] I felt unloved
- [ ] I felt judged
- [ ] I felt ignored
- [ ] I felt uncared for
- [ ] I felt forgotten
- [ ] I felt misunderstood
- [ ] I felt controlled

Mad As Hell

Action Questions

When I Get Angry

Place an X mark on all your anger warning signs

develops a headache	hearts start beating fast
yell and scream	stomach aches
body starts shaking	starts crying
throwing things	starts sweating
starts cussing	loses train of thought
gets quiet and shuts down	post messages on social media

Why do you do that? Have you always done that when you get angry?

_____
_____
_____

Mad As Hell

Action Questions

If you never let go of your anger towards the person that rejected you, how will it affect the rest of your life? How will it affect the life of the person that rejected you?

_____
_____
_____
_____
_____
_____
_____
_____

If you have not expressed your anger to the person that rejected you, is it possible for you to express your anger to them now? Do you want to express your anger to them?

_____
_____
_____
_____
_____
_____
_____
_____
_____
_____
_____

Mad As Hell

Action Questions

If you cannot express your anger to them, are you okay with that?

_____
_____
_____
_____
_____
_____

What do you need to do in order to release the anger?

_____
_____
_____
_____
_____
_____

What can you look forward to once you release the anger?

_____
_____
_____
_____
_____
_____
_____
_____

Mad As Hell

Prayer

Dear Heavenly Father,

Thank you for Your unconditional love that You graciously bestow on me each and every day. Though I fall short of Your glory every day, You love me anyways! And what a blessing that it is! Blessed it be Your Name!

Today I come to you because I need help overcoming my anger towards the person that rejected me. While I have the right to be angry with them, I do not have the right to use it as an excuse to sin or cause hurt and harm against them.

Lord, please forgive me for not expressing my anger righteously. I admit I need help controlling my temper. Teach me how to overlook an offense and use patience and wisdom when responding to others when I am mad.

Because You are watching over Your Word to perform it (Jeremiah 1:12), I am asking You to change my heart (Proverbs 21:1) towards them. Help me stop viewing them through the lens of my pain, and open my eyes so I can see them through the eyes of Your grace, love, mercy, and forgiveness.

Thank You Lord for being the greatest example on how to manage my anger. For You are slow to anger, always filled with unfailing love, forgiving every kind of sin and rebellion (Psalm 103:8). I pray that You give me the power and strength to model this behavior and characteristics daily.

In Your Son Jesus Name, I pray. Amen

Why Me

"You have circled this mountain long enough; turn northward."
-Deuteronomy 2:3

Why Me
Why Bother

Finally, I was going to get closure. As I drove up to Ex-Mr. Perfect's driveway, my mind started racing. A million questions started formulating in my head, but the only question I really wanted answered was, "Why me?" I wanted to know why did he pursue me if he knew he was only going to break my heart later?

Anger began to rise inside of my chest as I meditated upon that question. Why?! My thoughts kept raging until Ex-Mr. Perfect answered the door. His beautiful smile and warm embrace instantly melted away all of my anger.

"Hey, beautiful girl," he said as I walked inside. "Hey," I nervously replied. He was delighted to see me. I, on the other hand, was on a mission...a mission to get closure. I had no desire to get back with him. Yes, I still loved him, but I knew he was not a changed man. Though he tried several times after the relationship ended to convince me that he was, I knew he wasn't. Our ship had sailed, yet I still wanted "closure."

No matter what he tried to say or do, I had to remember my mission. Like the back of my hand, I knew him, so I already knew that he had everything planned for us. As always, he picked out a comedy movie for us to watch because he knew I liked comedies.

We tried to watch the movie, but the excitement of us seeing each other overruled it. The movie watched us as we talked, laughed, and reminisced over old times. Ex-Mr. Perfect's charm was becoming hard to resist. I knew he wanted us to get back together, but I just wanted closure.

Why Me

My opportunity came when he attempted to kiss me, and I blurted out, "Why did you break my heart?" Before I knew it, that one question turned into many as I lost track of how many I had asked.

Finally, he interrupted my line of questioning and said, "Oh, that's why you came?" Suddenly, his beautiful smile turned into a frown. "I'm sorry, Amber. I am really sorry that I hurt you." I thought once I heard those words from him, it would give me a sense of peace. Instead, it did the opposite. The anger that I had in the car filled my chest again.

"Why did you break my heart? Why did you choose me? Why me?!" The questions kept coming. It was like I couldn't stop. Tears began flowing from my eyes like rain drops. As I looked into his eyes, I saw remorse. He wiped my tears with his hand, but his mouth said no words. This was not the closure I had imagined in my head. I was asking all the right questions, but he was giving me no answers.

After a long silence, he finally said, "I'm sorry" and tried to kiss me again. I pushed him off me. At that moment, he knew any chance of us getting back together was over. So, we sat there in silence. I got my closure, but I didn't feel any better.

He said he was sorry, and he seemed like he genuinely meant it. But, if "sorry" was all I was going to get, why did I even bother seeking closure in the first place?

Why Me This Way

Here I am once again left in the dust
by a man I thought I could trust.
I just want to know why.
Was everything you ever told me a lie?
Why can't I just get over you and be free?
Free from the lies, the pain, the hurt, and the misery?
Like a broken record, I keep replaying our relationship over and over again in my head.
Thoughts of you and I keep me paralyzed in my bed.
What can I do? What can I say?
Why does our ending have to be this way?
For you and I to reconcile is what I pray,
but it doesn't look like it's going to happen today.

Why Me

What is closure? According to Webster's Dictionary, it's "an often comforting or satisfying sense of finality." I like how that particular definition says, "comforting or satisfying," but is closure really ever comforting? Or satisfying? I would definitely say not. But what is true in that definition is it is a "sense of finality." Once you get closure, it's really over.

After the ending of a relationship, the next phase is usually closure. This is the phase when both parties speak their peace and decide to go their separate ways. Normally, one or both parties apologize for the hurt they may have caused the other. After apologies are issued and accepted, both parties say their last goodbyes and wish each other well.

In a perfect world that would be the perfect way to have closure, but we don't live in a perfect world. And the even harsher reality is most people never receive closure. When we are rejected, we want answers. We want the dreaded question, "Why me?" answered. "Why did you not choose me? Why did you not love me? Why did you leave me? Why?"

In our minds, once those questions are answered, we can finally receive closure and accept the ending of the relationship. But what if the person who rejected you never tells you why? Could you still move on? The question should not be so much could you? But, when will you? When will you let go of the bitterness, anger, and sadness you are harboring in your heart towards the person that rejected you?

Why Me

How long will you keep crying yourself to sleep every night? How long will you keep stalking their social media pages and consuming yourself with their every move? How long will you keep asking yourself, "Why me?"

It would be great to know why, but, honestly, would knowing why someone didn't want you really help you feel better? Would that make the pain of them rejecting you hurt any less? Sometimes, you have to move on without the why.

The person who rejected you has already moved on. They have gone on with their lives, but you are still stuck, frozen in time hoping that they will unthaw you by giving you closure. Maybe, they will. Maybe, they won't. Regardless if they do or don't, you have to begin the process of moving on without them and without their why.

There is a time to cry and grieve, but after a certain amount of time, you got to get up, wash your face, and accept the reality that the relationship has ended. I understand that it's hard to let go of a relationship that you have invested a lot of love and time into, but you have to let the relationship and the person go.

It is natural to want to know why someone chooses to end a relationship with you, or if there was anything you could have done (or still can do) to make them change their minds. As natural as those thoughts are, you have to face the truth that they chose not to be with you and make the relationship work.

The sooner you are able to accept that, the sooner you will be able to heal and let the relationship go gracefully. Holding onto "why" will only leave you stuck in pain and misery.

 Why Me

Give yourself the gift of no longer waiting for closure from the person who rejected you. Take your life off hold and take your power back. If you want the "comforting and satisfy" closure the dictionary describes, you are going to have to give it to yourself. It is time for you to stop asking, "Why me?" and ask yourself, "Why am I holding on?" It is time to move on. It is time to let go.

Why Me
The Love I Never Had

How can I lose the love I never had?
So why am I so sad?
You never gave me your love, so in essence, I didn't lose anything.
So silly of me to think that you were really going to give me a ring.
Our eight months together meant nothing,
so why does it feel like I am missing something?
I guess it's my fault because I saw you through my limited perception.
So, I will take the blame for your deception.
In reality, I deceived myself, because I can't lose something I never had.
So why am I so sad?

Why Me
Circumstance Questions

Do you want closure from the person that rejected you?
_____
_____
_____

Do you think getting closure from the person that rejected you is important? Why or why not?
_____
_____
_____
_____
_____

Do you still want to be with the person that rejected you? Why or why not?
_____
_____
_____
_____
_____

Are you having a hard time moving on? Why do you feel like you are having a hard time?
_____
_____
_____
_____
_____
_____
_____

Why Me

Thought Questions

What thoughts come into your mind when you think about the person who rejected you?

Why do you feel the relationship ended?

Why are you unable to let the relationship go and move on?

Why Me

Thought Questions

Have you ever been rejected prior to this recent rejection? When and by who?

_____
_____
_____
_____
_____
_____
_____
_____
_____
_____
_____
_____

Have you ever rejected someone before? When and who?

_____
_____
_____
_____
_____
_____
_____
_____
_____
_____
_____
_____

Do you think of yourself as a victim? If so, why do you think of yourself a victim?

_____
_____
_____
_____
_____
_____
_____
_____
_____
_____

Do you miss the relationship or being in a relationship?

_____
_____
_____
_____
_____
_____
_____
_____
_____
_____

Why Me

Thought Questions

Why Me

Put a check mark by the statements that resonate with you.

- ☐ Why am I not good enough?

- ☐ Why did they not choose me?

- ☐ Why did they not love me?

- ☐ Why did they leave me?

What story do you tell yourself and others about the rejection? Is it true?

_____
_____
_____
_____
_____

What if the person that rejected you never tells you why? Could you still move on?

_____
_____
_____
_____
_____

Why Me

Feeling Questions

What feelings do you now feel towards the person that rejected you?

_____
_____
_____
_____
_____

What emotions are you holding on to towards the person that rejected you that you need to release?

_____
_____
_____
_____
_____

When will you let go of all of the emotions you are harboring in your heart towards the person that rejected you?

_____
_____
_____
_____
_____
_____

Why Me
Action Questions

Have you made the decision that this relationship is over?

_____
_____
_____
_____
_____

Have you stalked their social media pages? If so, has this helped you in your healing process or only consumed you with their every move?

_____
_____
_____
_____
_____

Have you ever given yourself closure before? What did that process look like?

_____
_____
_____
_____
_____
_____
_____

Why Me

Action Questions

If you received closure, how would it make you feel?

_____
_____
_____
_____
_____
_____
_____
_____
_____
_____

If you never receive closure, will you be okay with that? Why or why not?

_____
_____
_____
_____
_____
_____
_____
_____
_____
_____
_____
_____
_____

Why Me

Prayer

Dear Heavenly Father,

I will bless Your name at all times and Your praise shall continually be in my mouth (Psalm 34:1). Father You said, if I ask anything according to Your will, You will hear me (1 John 5:14).

Lord, please give me the strength to move on from the rejection and let go of the pain. You declare in Your Word that You will produce good from everything that happens to me because I love You and I have been called according to Your purpose (Romans 8:28).

Father, open my spiritual eyes of understanding, so I can see the good the rejection has produced in my life. Help me stop dwelling on what could and should have been.

You said in Your Word, "They went out from us, but they did not really belong to us. For if they had belonged to us, they would have remained with us; but their going showed that none of them belonged to us" (1 John 2:19).

Holy Spirit, help me grasp the revelation that the person that rejected me was never meant to stay in my life permanently. The relationship was just for a season, but it served a purpose. Reveal to me what that purpose was so I can let the relationship go in peace.

I ask all these things in Your Son Jesus name. Amen

Maybe, Maybe Not

"For every person will have to bear with patience his own burden of faults and shortcomings for which he alone is responsible."
- Galatians 6:5

Maybe, Maybe Not

It's Me, Not You

It is great to have friends who you can vent to and express your inner most thoughts and feelings. But what is even better is having friends who will tell you the truth about yourself when you are wrong.

The Bible says in Proverbs 27:6, "You can trust a friend who wounds you with his honesty." When you are going through a breakup the last thing you want to hear is your friends telling you that the person who dumped you did the right thing. Well, that is exactly what my friends were telling me, and I didn't want to hear it. Yes, I had my faults. I could openly and honestly admit that, but the ending of the relationship was my fault? How could they dare say such things to me, especially when I was grieving the loss of the relationship?

Okay, well, at this point, it had been three months since the breakup had happened, so I guess their patience with my little pity party had run out, but still…! The truth is a hard pill to swallow when you prefer chewing on lies.

In my mind, I was the one rejected. I was the one dumped. I was the one who had been left, so hearing about the mistakes that I made in the relationship, or things I should not have said or done wasn't what I wanted to hear. Yet, it was what I needed to hear. I needed to hear that I was inconsistent, selfish, and inconsiderate. Hearing those words was a reality check for me. It had been so easy for me to blame my ex for the ending of our relationship.

Maybe, Maybe Not

Lord knows, he had his fair share of issues, but the biggest issue in our relationship was me. I guess the saying is true... hurt people hurt people, and when he and I first got together, I was hurt. I still had bitterness in my heart towards the last person I dated before him, and I took that bitterness out on him. Though he tried to put up with me and my icy cold ways, he was tired!

Relationships are a two-way street, but he was on a one-way, and I was simply on the side of the road watching him drive. I loved him, but I was never truly in love with him. He was a great guy, but the connection just wasn't there for me. In retrospection, I only got with him to make the last guy I dated jealous. So, yes, my friends were right; I was selfish. I was mad because he broke up with me, not realizing it broke his heart to do so.

It took my friends to bust my bubble and make me get off my high horse to admit how selfish and inconsiderate I was to him throughout the relationship. Now, he was no saint either, but he didn't deserve to keep putting up with my cold treatment towards him. He deserved better. He deserved someone who was willing to love, respect, and cherish him. Something I was simply incapable and unwilling to do.

It took me three months to come to that realization. Prior to that, I had been grieving over the breakup and telling anyone who would listen about how he did me wrong. Well, I was the one who was wrong. I was wrong for even getting into a relationship with him in the first place. When relationships end, it is human nature to single one person out for the bulk of the blame. But the truth is everybody shares some.

Maybe, Maybe Not

Deep down in his heart, he knew I wasn't over the last guy I dated, so we started the relationship on a bad foundation. We were never on the same page.

The Bible says in Amos 3:3, "Can two people walk together without agreeing on the direction?" He and I were never walking in the same direction. Maybe, I was to blame for the end of the relationship, or, maybe, he just didn't pick up on the signs. Either way, the relationship ended, and we both had to move on.

Maybe, I Changed

You say I've changed, and maybe I have, but what about you?
You try to put all the blame on me, but you share some too.
For years, I tried to make it work, but you never met me halfway.
Now, you're asking me why I have nothing left to say.
I am done trying.
I am tired of you lying.
No more words, no more tears.
I don't care about your investment and all these years.
I give up; I throw in the towel.
I just want to be single for a while.
It's not about someone else.
I just want to be by myself.
Maybe, I have changed; maybe, I'm the reason why our relationship is ending.
You can blame me all you want to, but I am done pretending.
It is time for us to go our separate ways and embark on new beginnings.

Maybe, Maybe Not

When someone decides that they no longer want you to be a part of their life, it's easy to think negatively about yourself. Someone's rejection of you is not a reflection of your self-worth. The sooner your broken heart can accept this, the quicker it will heal. It will also heal quicker if you quit meditating on thoughts like, If only I would have done this or that. What did I do wrong? Was there something I could've said or done to make them change their mind? They should have done this or that.

Thoughts like that keep you stuck playing the blame game—the game where we decide the person responsible for the demise of the relationship. What I have learned about the blame game is no matter who is responsible it won't change the fact that the relationship is over. Maybe, you were to blame; maybe, you were not. Regardless of who is at fault, both parties are responsible for learning from the experience.

I have often heard people say the relationships we have with other people mirrors the relationship we have with ourselves. When we are in-tune with ourselves and self-aware of our thoughts, feelings, actions, and behaviors, we can rationalize the end of relationships objectively.

Rejection is painful, but rejection can be our teacher if we sit and become its student. When we are self-aware we can recognize when our mind is creating fake stories about the rejection. We cannot always control the thoughts that come into our heads, but we can control how long they stay there, and which ones take root and influence how we feel and, ultimately, what we say and do.

Maybe, Maybe Not

Being self-aware also helps us recognize the only person we are responsible for figuring out or changing is ourselves. And what a job that it is! When we focus on ourselves, we don't have time to psychoanalyze the person who rejected us. Just like us, they have their own needs, wants, desires, and rights as an individual, including the right to discontinue a relationship with us.

Restlessly obsessing over why they made that choice is counterproductive. Maybe, they had needs you couldn't meet, or maybe they felt like they couldn't meet yours.

Maybe, they felt a lack of connection with you. Maybe, they wanted something more casual, and you wanted something more serious or vice versa. Maybe, they just weren't the right person for you. I know you would love for them to tell you the reason why they rejected you.

Regardless if they do or don't, move on anyway. When someone tells you that they don't love you or want to be with you, don't chase behind them trying to change their minds. Why do you want to be in a relationship with someone who has expressed to you that they don't want you? Why waste time trying to convince someone of your worth and value?

Instead of begging, playing games, and fighting with them to prove your worth, let them go and work on healing yourself. Let go of the burden of trying to force love. The love that you deserve and need will be freely given to you. Rejection opens the door for that love to find you.

Maybe, Maybe Not

While you can't figure them out, you can examine yourself and address any negative behaviors you contributed to the relationship. One of the signs of a mature person is their ability to see and acknowledge their own toxic thoughts and behaviors. Maybe, you were the reason the relationship ended. Own that fact.

Assess the role you played in the rejection and hold yourself accountable for your problematic thoughts and behaviors. There is beauty in being self-aware and honest with yourself. As you tell yourself the truth, you will receive clarity in areas of your life that you need to improve in. You will also make room for healing, growth, and evolution. Don't allow self-deception to delay this process.

Sometimes, rejection is God's protection and redirection, and, sometimes it's the result of our own doing. Sometimes, the best thing a person can do for you is reject you. There is no sense of wanting to be in a relationship with someone who doesn't want or value you. Nor does it make sense for you to keep projecting your past hurts and pain onto innocent people. Stop playing the blame game and accept the fact that relationship is over. Learn the lessons.

Maybe, Maybe Not
Another Sad Love Song

Rejection is a painful thing to feel.
Rejection cuts at the heart, and the heart is a hard thing to heal.
I have been rejected many times in my life, and I have rejected others too.
But the worse rejection I have ever felt was the rejection from you.
You say it's not me. That you need some space.
So why couldn't you tell me this face-to-face?
You say it's not about someone else.
You just need to be by yourself.
You break my heart through a text,
leaving me clueless on what to do next.
You say I was the perfect girl, and you don't deserve me.
And all you want now is for me to be happy.
But I was happy with you.
And I thought you were happy with me too.
Maybe, I was wrong.
I guess I will just play another sad love song.

Maybe, Maybe Not

Circumstance Questions

Did you have time to prepare for the ending of the relationship or did it happen all of a sudden?

_____
_____
_____
_____
_____
_____

Do you still have questions about why the relationship ended?

_____
_____
_____
_____
_____
_____

Who do you think is the blame for the relationship's ending?

_____
_____
_____
_____
_____
_____
_____
_____
_____
_____

―― Maybe, Maybe Not ――

Thought Questions

What negative thought patterns or beliefs systems about the rejection do you need to let go of that are no longer serving you?

Are you having trouble moving past this rejection because of other rejections you have experienced in the past?

What are some things that you need to hear from your support system that you do not want to hear, but need to hear?

Maybe, Maybe Not

Thought Questions

In retrospective, were there any red flags in the beginning of the relationship that you overlooked?

Was it possible that you projected issues from past relationships into the relationship with the person that rejected you?

Were there any problems in the relationships?

— Maybe, Maybe Not —

Thought Questions

Did you make any mistakes in the relationship that you still repeatedly blame yourself for?

What regrets do you have about the relationship itself or the way it ended? If you could have a do-over for the ending, what would you do differently?

Thoughts/Feeling Questions

Relationship Reflection

What emotions did you display in the relationship? Were you negative or positive in the relationship? Describe in detail the emotions you projected throughout the relationship.

_____
_____
_____
_____
_____
_____
_____
_____
_____
_____

How did you emotionally deal with conflicts within the relationship? How did the other person emotionally deal with conflicts within the relationship?

_____
_____
_____
_____
_____
_____
_____
_____
_____
_____
_____

― Maybe, Maybe Not ―

Thoughts/Feeling Questions

Relationship Reflection

Do you think that the relationship started off on a strong foundation?

_____
_____
_____
_____
_____
_____

Honestly, do you feel like the person that rejected you was the right person for you or did you settle with being with them?

_____
_____
_____
_____
_____
_____
_____
_____

Did the person that rejected you have any negative flaws or traits? If so, what were they? Did you address those traits with them?

_____
_____
_____
_____
_____
_____
_____

Maybe, Maybe Not

Thoughts/Feeling Questions

Relationship Reflection

Did the person that rejected you push you to be a better person?	Yes / No
Did your life improve by being with the person?	Yes / No
Did you push them to be a better person?	Yes / No
Do you think you helped them improve their life?	Yes / No
Do you think you gave a 100% in the relationship?	Yes / No
Do you they think they gave a 100% in the relationship?	Yes / No

Action Questions

Are you ready to release this relationship and move into a new phase in your life?

_____
_____
_____
_____

What action steps are you taking to move forward and let this relationship go? (Ex. Seeking Counseling, Praying, etc.)

_____
_____
_____
_____
_____
_____
_____

What did you learn from this relationship that you will take into your next relationship?

_____
_____
_____
_____
_____
_____
_____
_____
_____

Maybe, Maybe Not

Action Questions

Did you observe any negative patterns or traits about yourself during the relationship? What traits did you notice and how will you fix them?

_____
_____
_____
_____
_____
_____
_____
_____
_____

Since the relationship has ended, do you feel like you have grown as a person? In what ways have you grown? How are you expressing this growth in your current relationships?

_____
_____
_____
_____
_____
_____
_____
_____
_____
_____

Maybe, Maybe Not

Prayer

Dear Heavenly Father,

Thank You for being such a loving and merciful Father. I honor, praise, and glorify Your name. You are great and greatly to be praised!

Lord, look deep within my heart and examine all my motives and thoughts (Psalm 7:9). Reveal to me my hidden sins and faults.

Lord, maybe I was the reason for the rejection. Maybe, I was not. Either way, I know there are some character traits I can improve on. Holy Spirit, show me the areas I need to work on.

No longer will I blame the person that rejected me, I will evaluate myself and do the inner work in my heart, soul, mind, and spirit. Help me Lord to glorify You in my words, actions, and works.

I ask these things in Your Son Jesus name. Amen

Choosing To Forgive You

"And whenever you
stand praying, if you find that
you carry something in your heart
against another person, release him
and forgive him so that your
Father in heaven will also release you
and forgive you of your faults."
—Mark 11:25

Choosing To Forgive You
Releasing His Debt

As I sat on the edge of my bed, I took a deep breath and sent the text. I couldn't believe I was actually texting him. It had been almost two years since I had last spoken with him, but all I could think about was the last time I saw his face at my house. His beautiful brown eyes mesmerized my soul as he got into his car to drive off.

The longing we felt for each other was unbearable. Our last hug seemed to last forever. No words needed to be spoken. The love was still there. But that love was interrupted by the reality that he was married. A reality he neglected to tell me as he sat next to me on my living room couch, staring into my eyes and holding my hand.

As I waited on him to respond, I kept replaying that scene in my head. I had to think of the love I once felt for him to subdue the anger that was rising in my heart. It wasn't my idea to text him. If it was up to me, I would've never spoken to him again. But God wasn't having it. He told me the night before that I had to text him and apologize to him for reaching out to his wife and telling her about our encounter.

Naturally, I resisted the command. I knew that I needed to take accountability and apologize for my actions, but needing to and wanting to are two different things. Hell, he hadn't even apologized to me for his antics, yet God wanted me to be the bigger person.

I was tired of being the bigger person. He knew he was married when he came over my house. He could have told me, but he didn't. He wanted the temporary fantasy, but I deserved the truth.

Choosing To Forgive You

As my mind pondered these thoughts, my phone started vibrating. He texted back. I knew he would. He had called me a few months prior, but I didn't answer. I'm sure he was surprised to hear from me. His response was nice and cordial. He accepted my apology and even said he hoped that I was "doing well." But what he didn't do was take responsibility for the pain and offense he had caused me.

Immediately after reading his text, I got angry and threw my phone down. He was still trying to pretend that he just came over "to get a book". After all the time that had passed, that was his excuse. I thought I had forgiven him, but, in that moment, God showed me that I still held offense against him in my heart. I thought I was over it, but nope, the wound was still fresh. I guess time does not heal all wounds.

I sat on the edge of my bed and cried. I knew I had to restart the forgiveness process over again. I just knew for sure once I issued my apology he was going to issue his. So, when he didn't I was crushed. I was disappointed beyond measure. Yet, I learned a valuable lesson that day.

My forgiveness of someone should never be predicated upon their remorse or even their acknowledgment of their wrongdoing. Whether they are sorry or not, I have to forgive them anyway. That day, I chose to forgive him from his debt of an apology. I guess that was the lesson God wanted me to learn all along.

Choosing To Forgive You
Struggle to Forgive

You broke my heart; you hurt me so bad.
I am trying to forgive you, but I am still mad.
You want to talk to me; you want us to remain friends,
but I don't think we can.
You left me for another woman, and, now, you want to come back.
The audacity to think you got it like that.
Where were you when I cried every night, wishing for you to return?
Remembering your last words and listening to Usher's "Let It Burn".
Well, I'm still coping with your heartless goodbye,
so I don't think I have it in me to give it another try.
I'm still struggling to forgive you, though I am trying.
But I can't seem to hear your voice or look at your face without crying.

Choosing To Forgive You

The relationship has ended and the person that rejected you has moved on with their life. The way they ended the relationship with you was cruel. Maybe, they ended the relationship by ghosting you, or maybe, you found out from another source that they were cheating on you.

Either way, they didn't have the decency or respect for you to tell you face-to-face that they didn't want to be with you anymore. You feel like they owe you an apology, but do they?

When someone rejects you, they do not owe you an apology. They have the right as a human being to change their minds about you anytime they want. No matter how painful it may be for you, they don't have to apologize for their choice to end a relationship with you.

However, if they ended the relationship in an insensitive manner or with no consideration of how their rejection would affect you mentally and emotionally, they do owe you an apology. They owe you an apology because of the way they ended the relationship, not because they ended it. Please, understand the difference.

If someone ends a relationship with you in a respectful manner, they don't owe you an apology. Yes, I know the rejection hurt your feelings, but hurt feelings don't constitute the need for an apology.

On the contrary, if the way they ended the relationship was with a lack of compassion or concern for your feelings, then, yes, you have the right to be offended, and they should apologize. But just because they should doesn't mean they will.

Choosing To Forgive You

More than likely, they probably will never apologize to you. Be honest, have you ended all of your relationships, personally and professionally, on a good note? Did you always consider the feelings of the other people involved?

I know I haven't. I've quit jobs before and didn't even tell my employers, and I've ghosted a couple of men in my past who I lost interest in. I know I've caused pain and offense to a lot of people I have ended relationships with, intentionally and unintentionally.

In retrospection, I wish I could go back and change the way I chose to handle the ending of those relationships, but I can't...neither can the person who rejected you change the bad way they chose to end things with you, so what do you do?

What do you do when you are owed an apology, but the person who owes it to you chooses not to give it to you? Do you villainize the offender? Do you hold your healing contingent upon them telling you that they're sorry? Do you stay stuck in pain and turmoil?

No, you make a decision to forgive them anyway. Forgiveness isn't a feeling; it's a choice. A choice you make because you deserve peace and freedom from the pain that you are harboring in your heart. I know forgiving them will be hard, but you have to, so you can be free and heal. Forgive them even if they're not sorry or never apologize to you. Forgiveness is for you; it's not for them.

While receiving an apology would be nice, you can move forward without one. Don't hold yourself hostage waiting on an apology. Forgiveness is a process that takes time. It takes you fully accepting that the relationship is over and that the person who hurt you may or may not apologize.

Choosing To Forgive You

I have learned through my own personal experiences with rejection that some of the people that rejected me had absolutely no remorse over the way they chose to end our relationship. They didn't care that I was hurt or offended. They intentionally ended their relationship with me in a heartless way. Not only that, they moved on with their life as if they never even knew me. Talk about coldhearted!

Yet, in spite of their actions, I chose to forgive them anyways. Forgiveness is a choice, and your healing is dependent upon your choice to forgive. If the person who rejected you did it in a respectful way, awesome. You just have to accept the fact that the relationship is over, grieve it, learn the lessons it came to teach you, and move on. If the person who rejected you didn't end the relationship with you in a respectful manner, and you're offended by it, you have to make a choice today to forgive them.

Choosing To Forgive You
On the Other Foot

I forgive you, but I pray you can forgive me.
I know I am the cause of your unhappiness and misery.
If I can take back the hurt I caused you, I would.
How badly I wish I could.
They say, "two wrongs don't make a right."
Well, I didn't care that night.
Now, look at the damage my selfish act has caused.
I know I am at fault, but I hope we can come to a peaceful resolve.
This time it's me asking for forgiveness, so now, I know how you feel.
I hope time gives us both closure so our hearts can heal.

Choosing To Forgive You
Qualification Questions

If you have already forgiven the person that rejected you, you can skip this phase of questions. If the person that rejected you did it respectfully, you may also skip these questions.

Based on the phase overview, do you fall into the category of deserving an apology or needing to let it go?

_____
_____
_____
_____
_____
_____
_____
_____

If you feel that you deserve an apology, have you received one?

_____
_____
_____
_____
_____
_____
_____
_____

If you have not received an apology, do you still feel like you are owed one? Why or why not?

_____
_____
_____
_____
_____
_____
_____
_____

Did the person that rejected you take your feelings inconsideration when they ended the relationship with you?

_____
_____
_____
_____
_____
_____
_____
_____

Choosing To Forgive You

Circumstance Questions

Have you forgiven the person that rejected you? Why or why not?

_____
_____
_____
_____
_____
_____

Do you want to forgive the person that rejected you? Are you emotionally ready to forgive them?

_____
_____
_____
_____

Have you done anything to the person that rejected you that you need to ask them forgiveness for? What did you do and why did you do it?

_____
_____
_____
_____
_____
_____
_____
_____
_____
_____

Choosing To Forgive You

Circumstance Questions

Do you have the capacity to reach out to them and ask them for forgiveness?

___

Have you asked them for forgiveness? Why or why not?

___

If they never forgive you, will you be okay with that?

___

Choosing To Forgive You

Thought Questions

What are the major offenses that you hold against the person that rejected you? Is it the way they rejected you or the fact that they rejected you?

Why do you think you are owed an apology?

What will an apology do for you in relation to your healing?

Choosing To Forgive You

Feeling Questions

Does not forgiving the person make you feel good? Does it make you feel in control? How does withholding forgiveness benefit you? How does it benefit them?

_____
_____
_____
_____
_____
_____
_____
_____
_____

What is the hardest part emotionally about forgiving the person that rejected you?

_____
_____
_____
_____
_____
_____
_____
_____
_____

Choosing To Forgive You

Feelings/Action Questions

How Is Unforgiveness Affecting You

Put a check mark by any of the examples that apply to you.

☐ Emotional instability (e.g. anger or shame)

☐ Changed mindset (e.g. recurring thoughts about rejection: I am not lovable, I am worthless)

☐ Social isolation (e.g. avoiding new relationships)

☐ Not open to change (e.g. injuries from abuse)

☐ Physical health (e.g. recurring viruses or infections)

☐ Spiritual health (e.g. Hardened heart, decrease in prayer life)

Describe in detail how the checked examples are affecting you. Feel free to add something else that wasn't listed.

_____
_____
_____
_____
_____
_____
_____

Choosing To Forgive You

Action Questions

If you choose not to forgive the person that rejected you, what do you think the consequences are going to be? ex. missing opportunities, not allowing love in, holding on to things to long (i.e. holding grudges)

_____
_____
_____
_____
_____
_____
_____
_____

How would forgiving the person that rejected you positively impact your life?

_____
_____
_____
_____
_____
_____
_____
_____

Choosing To Forgive You

Action Questions

Forgiveness Activation

Speak the forgiveness activation out loud as many times as you need to until you feel like you have finally forgiven the person that rejected you.

I forgive ————————————————————

and I choose to move on and let them go in peace.

I forgive ————————————————————

not because they deserve it, but because I deserve

to be at peace and free from suffering and pain.

I will give forgiveness by

_____
_____
_____

I forgive myself for

_____
_____
_____

I accept responsibility for any negative or hurtful things I said or did to ————————————————

I will ask them for their forgiveness.

Choosing To Forgive You

Prayer

Dear Heavenly Father,

You are a great an awesome God and I give You the praise, honor, and glory due to Your name.

Father You said if I don't forgive others, You will not forgive me (Matthew 6:35). I want to forgive the person that rejected me, but I am struggling. They ended the relationship with me in a dishonorable way and I am still carrying a spirit of offense against them for it. Help me to release the offense so I will not develop a root bitterness in my heart towards them (Hebrews 12:15).

Because I have been graciously forgiven by You, I must release this same gift of forgiveness to them. I will make allowance for their offense and give it You for You to deal with. As I release this offense to You, I now have the freedom to walk in total peace. God, bless them and give them peace too.

I ask these things in Your Son Jesus name. Amen

It Is What Is

"No, dear brothers, I am still not all I should be, but I am bringing all my energies to bear on this one thing: Forgetting the past and looking forward to what lies ahead."
-Philippians 3:13

It What It Is

Birthday Lessons

I thought my 30th birthday was epic, but it had nothing on my 31st! On August 31st, 2018, I took a one day road trip with one of my best friends to Memphis, Tennessee. I had planned the trip for an entire month, and when the day finally came I was ready to go!

I got up early that morning and just basked in the day. The year before I spent my birthday on a cruise, and I had an absolute blast! It was my first cruise, and I loved it. For my 31st birthday, I wanted to do a road trip and explore one of my favorite towns. And that we did! We went to every mall in the city. I spent so much money in H&M it was ridiculous! I had never shopped in an H&M store before, and I lost my mind while I was there. The clothes were so cute and affordable.

After shopping half the day away, we ate at Huey's restaurant in Midtown, and then we visited the Stax Museum and the National Civil Rights Museum. The exhibits were powerful, especially the ones at the Stax Museum. Many of the exhibits featured Aretha Franklin, whose funeral was going on at the same time we were visiting. It was a very emotional experience for me and my friend, but I'm glad that we got to visit the museum and learn about her legacy, as well as the legacies of many other black soul artists.

After browsing the museums, we went to another mall, and then, finally, we went to the B.B. King's Blues Club. As we sat and listened to the sounds of the performer on stage singing Otis Redding's song "Try a Little Tenderness," Ex-Mr. Perfect messaged me on Instagram.

It What It Is

"I have a present for you." I knew the present he was offering me was not something I wanted to receive. Same ole Ex-Mr. Perfect, but, this time, I was a different Amber. Instead of getting mad, I laughed and messaged him back, "Thank You!"

We messaged each other back and forth for about an hour until I finally made it clear that I had no desire to see him. Unfortunately for him, he wasn't going to get to see me in my birthday suit! I think he knew it, but he tried to shoot his shot anyway.

It felt good to hold a conversation with him without either one of us getting overly emotional. Normally, when we talked, we would get into an argument within five minutes of the conversation.

After our breakup, we became like oil and water. We just did not mix anymore. We tried the whole "being cool" thing, but he thought that meant that we were back together. We just could not get on the same page, but that night, it was different.

That night, we didn't argue. Ex-Mr. Perfect was his snarky self, but I didn't let him agitate me. Plus, it was my birthday. Who wants to get into it with someone on their birthday? So, I just let it ride and enjoyed talking to him in the moment.

At some point, I had to let all of the animosity I felt towards him go. That night, I let it go. I accepted that the rejection happened to me, but it didn't define who I was.

It What It Is

Since our breakup, I had excelled in my life. I graduated from graduate school, I started a ministry and a business, and I published a book. Life had treated me well, and life had treated him well too. We both had grown in different areas in our lives.

When I woke up the next morning, I got up and smiled. I had an amazing birthday, and I also reached a major milestone in my healing journey. I finally entered the acceptance phase! I realized that the rejection I once hated was one of my greatest blessings!

It What It Is

Life Goes On

Life goes on.
I have to stay strong,
even though you did me wrong.
I played with fire and I got burned.
No need to dwell on what happened; I take it as a lesson learned,
because life goes on.
I have to stay strong
for the relationships that will follow.
Giving myself hope for a better tomorrow.
I experienced pain,
but I also gained.
So, I'm no longer sad
or reminiscing on what we had,
because life goes on.
I have to stay strong.

It What It Is

The relationship is over. The person that rejected you has moved on. Now, it's time for you to do the same. Constantly feeling sad and angry about what happened will not change the past. Stop feeling guilty about what you could have done or should have done in the relationship.

Stop blaming yourself for being rejected. God allowed the rejection to happen for a reason, so let go of your lingering feelings of pain, shame, anger, guilt, longing, and resentment. Holding on to those feelings is a waste of valuable energy and time. Accept that the relationship is over and give yourself the permission to move on and stop reminiscing on what used to be.

Stop talking about it. Stop telling everybody what they did to you. Stop looking on their social media pages to see how they're doing. The rejection happened, but it's not the end of your life. Heal from it, accept it, and learn the lessons it came to teach you. Trust God, that He is working the rejection out for your good. Make peace with the person and make peace with the situation.

Once you do this, you are ready to move on. Acceptance is the final phase of healing from rejection. In the other phases, you worked through a variety of different feelings—sadness, self-pity, anger, regret, blame, etc. You processed those feelings. You felt them. You sat with them. You listened to them. Now, learn what they came to teach you.

The rejection doesn't have to become a painful memory in your past. It can be an opportunity for self-reflection and self-growth. There are many things you can learn about yourself after you heal from rejection.

It What It Is

Rejection is an indicator that something in your life is not working. Maybe, you need to develop a more positive mindset or work on your physical health. Use the lessons from the rejection as an opportunity to move forward in your life with greater clarity, gratitude, understanding, and wisdom.

When you accept the rejection, you will no longer feel its sting, and you will realize that the person that rejected you actually did you a favor. You are worth more than being somewhere with someone who doesn't want you. You deserve to be loved fully by someone who is capable and willing to love you like Christ loves the Church.

You deserve unconditional love. The person who rejected you simply couldn't give you that love, so stop chasing what you thought you had or what could have been and open your heart to the love that will be. Accept that the rejection happened, and it is what it is.

It What It Is

Never Meant To Be

I let you go; I set you free.
I have finally accepted that you and I are just not meant to be.
All the vows we made, our promises of forever,
are just words that mean nothing because you and I will never get back together.
Our love was like a fairytale, but then it abruptly ended.
Unlike the movies, our relationship cannot be mended,
so we go our separate ways.
From time to time, thinking about the days
when I used to love you, and you used to love me.
How in love we used to be.
But now, those days are just figments of our imagination.
Because we have both come to the realization
that we just weren't meant to be.

It What It Is

Circumstance Questions

Do you finally feel like you have accepted the rejection? Why or why not?

_____
_____
_____
_____
_____

Have you been in contact with the person that rejected you? If you have, why have you been in contact with that person?

_____
_____
_____
_____
_____
_____
_____
_____

Describe your interactions. Were they positive or negative?

_____
_____
_____
_____
_____
_____
_____
_____

It What It Is
Thought Questions

Are your thoughts usually in the past, present, or future?

What thought patterns are holding you back right now from accepting the rejection?

What lies are your inner critic telling you about the rejection that you need to let go of?

It What It Is

Thought Questions

What are you currently doing that no longer serves you in your healing journey?

What new realities has this rejection forced you to see about yourself?

■■■■ It What It Is ■■■■

Thought Questions

What strengths have you discovered about yourself as a result of this rejection? What weaknesses have you discovered about yourself as a result of this rejection?

In what ways have you grown after this rejection?

It What It Is

Thought Questions

What do you think this rejection came to teach you?

It What It Is

Feeling Questions

How are your emotions blocking you from accepting the rejection? What are some feelings you need to let go of?

_____
_____
_____
_____
_____
_____

Are you experiencing suffering as a result of not accepting the rejection?

_____
_____
_____
_____
_____
_____

What healthy emotions would you like to implement into your life?

_____
_____
_____
_____
_____
_____

▬▬▬ It What It Is ▬▬▬

Action Questions

In what ways have you given yourself permission to move on and think forward?

_____
_____
_____
_____
_____
_____

Are there any changes you are resisting to make in your life that will help you accept the rejection? What are those changes? Why have you not made them? When will you make them?

_____
_____
_____
_____
_____
_____
_____
_____
_____
_____
_____
_____
_____
_____

It What It Is

Action Questions

How can you set a thriving atmosphere to support you in your journey of healing? (ex. decluttering your space, redecorating, etc.)

_____
_____
_____
_____
_____
_____

What are some areas in your life that you would like to see improvement in? What steps can you implement starting today that will help you start seeing improvement?

_____
_____
_____
_____
_____
_____
_____
_____
_____
_____
_____
_____
_____

━━━ It What It Is ━━━

Action Questions

List three things you need to remove from your life to declutter your heart and mind.

_____
_____
_____
_____
_____
_____

When you accept the rejection, what are some things that you will be able to get back to doing that will cultivate more joy in your life?

_____
_____
_____
_____
_____
_____
_____
_____
_____
_____
_____
_____
_____
_____

━━━ It What It Is ━━━

Prayer

Dear Heavenly Father,

I praise You because You are the God of endings and new beginnings. Thank You for being with me throughout every season of my life.

Father, You said in Your Word, "There is a time for everything, and a season for every activity under the heavens" (Ecclesiastes 3:1). It is time for me to accept this rejection. I thank You for allowing the relationship to end because I know You have someone else better for me.

Holy Spirit, help me not to dwell on the rejection or remember the former pain. Starting this day forward, I will continually fix my thoughts on things that are "authentic and real, honorable and admirable, beautiful and respectful, pure and holy, merciful and kind...and on every glorious work of God, praising Him always" (Philippians 4:8).

I decree and declare that my mourning season is over! I leave the past behind and I press forward to the future You have planned for me.

I pray this in Your Son Jesus name. Amen

Give Me Time

"A time to destroy; A time to rebuild."
-Ecclesiastes 3:3

Give Me Time

Season of Rebuilding

Some people cry rivers, but I cry oceans. I hate crying, so when I do, I cry for hours. The day I made the decision to seek professional counseling, I cried for three hours straight. I woke up early on a Sunday morning and released years of pain in a soul wrenching crying session. With each tear that I cried, I gained strength and courage. My tears became the catalyst for a breakthrough. I knew that if I genuinely wanted to get healed from the rejections of my past, I needed to seek additional help.

Rejection was a reoccurring issue for me, particularly with men. Every man I truly ever loved rejected me. My father rejected me before I was even born, and I knew that his rejection was the root cause of my other rejections from men. Subconsciously, I chose men who mirrored the characteristics of my father. It was like through them I was trying to win the love and affection of my father.

I knew all of these revelations before my counselor confirmed them to me in our first session. When I told her that I already knew the root of my rejection, she said to me in a nice, but stern voice, "If you knew that already, why haven't you done anything about it?"

Crickets. I didn't have an answer for her. My counselor read me like a book and could see through my "strong girl" act. After what seemed like hours of silence, she smiled and said to me, "It's okay to know what your root issues are. In fact, it's good that you know that your rejection issues started with your father, but now that you know, what are you going to do about it?"

Give Me Time

I had the revelation on "why," but I didn't have a Blue's Clue on the "how". How was I going to stop this never-ending cycle of rejection in my life? She read me like a book again, answering my internal question. "Amber, we are going to have to tear down your foundation and rebuild it. You have allowed rejection to become a part of your identity, and that is why you keep attracting rejection in your life."

I looked at her with amazement after she said that. She was right! I did allow rejection to become a part of my identity. I wore it like a badge of honor. I called myself "the rejected girl". I believed because all I had ever experienced in relationships with men was rejection, betrayal, and heartache, that was all my experience with them would ever be. It was always about what they did to me, never realizing I had a role to play in my own rejections. Deep!

After I dropped my strong girl act, I allowed myself to become vulnerable with her and humbled myself. At the end of each session, she would give me a homework assignment and some book recommendations for me to read. Like Iyanla Vanzant, she said, "If you want to overcome the spirit of rejection, you got to 'do the work!'" I did my work!

I did nine sessions with my counselor, and by the end of the last session, I realized that while my father may have been the root of my rejection, I was the one still perpetuating it in my life. My lack of boundaries and victim mindset was the reason I allowed myself to deal with men I knew were incapable and unwilling to love me. I had to tear down the foundation of rejection in my life and rebuild a new foundation of love and acceptance. I had to do the work, and I am still doing the work today.

Give Me Time

Dear Heart

You are filled with so much love, but you have no one to give it to.
You have been broken, you have been crushed, but no matter what you go through,
you prevail, you heal, you remain strong,
no matter how or who did you wrong.
After picking you up so many times and putting you back together, I have realized that you are too delicate to be just given away.
No matter what my mind has to say.
I will listen to you, oh, heart...I will protect you and guard you the best that I can.
I will not give you away to just "any" man.
You will tell me where you should go,
and I will follow.
So, next time, before I start...
I will listen to you, my dear heart.

Give Me Time

The Bible declares that there is a time and season for everything (Ecclesiastes 3:1). In the beginning phases of your healing process, you spent time crying and lamenting. While that season was necessary, you are embarking on a new season.

In this season, it is time for you to tear down old and unhealthy thought patterns and behaviors and replace them with new and healthy ones. It is time for you to stop looking at the rejection and start looking inside yourself and seeing what areas in your life you need to heal and improve in.

Before you enter into a new relationship, you need to give yourself time to do the internal work in your mind, heart, soul, body, and spirit. Become the best version of you, so when real love comes along, you will be able to recognize and receive it.

The most important relationship you will ever have on this earth is the relationship you have with yourself. The relationship you have with yourself determines the outcome of every other relationship in your life. When someone rejects you, the relationship you have with yourself can become compromised. Rejection from others can also make you reject yourself.

One of the most damaging impacts rejection leaves on one's soul is the ability to make a person feel unloved and unlovable. While the person that rejected you may have made you feel unloved, you are not unlovable. You are worthy of love; they just were incapable of loving you.

Give Me Time

So, don't believe the lie that rejection tries to deposit in your mind. Uproot that lie and replace it with the truth of God's Word that you are fearfully and wonderfully made and worthy of His love and the love of others, but most importantly, the love of yourself.

It is time for you to release and redefine what love is and what is expected of you in order to give and receive it. There may be some things you need to work on, but that still doesn't disqualify you from receiving unconditional love. So, allow yourself the time you need to do the inner healing work, and show yourself love and grace as you go through the process.

When you break free from old mindsets, habits, patterns, defense mechanisms, and pain, be prepared to face mental and physical resistance from past lovers, friends, and even family members. Everyone will not embrace the new changes you are making in your life, and that's okay. When people are used to you behaving in a certain way, it can be hard for them to accept you acting and behaving differently.

That is understandable, but don't let their disapproval or reactions make you go back to your old ways of thinking and behaving. Don't silence your needs, wants, and feelings for the sake of keeping peace with others. Your needs, wants, and feelings are important, even if they're not met with the understanding, nurturing, and the love that they deserve.

Give Me Time

Everyone is not going to like the inner healing work you are doing, but keep doing it anyway. Give them, as well as yourself, time to come around and embrace the new changes, because it's time for you to tear down your old foundation and build a new one.

Give Me Time

I'm Ready

Lord, tear down my broken walls and build them back up again.
I am tired of losing in the area of love; I am ready to win.
I am ready to learn the lessons from my past relationships' endings.
I am ready to heal, so You can bring me new beginnings.
I give You full permission to come in and do a new work within me.
I am ready to let the past go and finally be happy.
Tear down these walls and build them back up again.
I am ready this time; let the process begin.

Give Me Time
Circumstance Questions

How do you feel about the rejection today?

_____
_____
_____
_____
_____
_____
_____
_____
_____
_____
_____

Since the rejection, how is the relationship with yourself?

_____
_____
_____
_____
_____
_____
_____
_____
_____
_____
_____
_____

Give Me Time
Thought Questions

What is your current mindset? Is it serving you? If it is not serving you, how can you change it to serve you?

Define what living authentically means to you. Are you living an authentic life? Why or why not? What prevents you from living an authentic life?

Give Me Time

Thought Questions

Do you feel like you are living the life you want or the life that others have projected onto you? (ex. Family, Friends, Society)

Do you compare yourself to others and how can you stop comparing yourself?

Give Me Time
Thought Questions

Make a list of three negative things you tell yourself, then write a second list to counteract each negative thing.

What are some positive and negative traits about yourself? And why did you pick these traits?

Give Me Time

Feeling Questions

What emotional needs were you trying to obtain from the person that rejected you that you could have filled yourself?

_____
_____
_____
_____
_____
_____
_____
_____
_____
_____
_____
_____

What are your greatest emotional needs in relationships? How do you feel when your needs aren't being met?

_____
_____
_____
_____
_____
_____
_____

Give Me Time

Feeling Questions

Do you struggle with being vulnerable? If you do, why do you struggle?

Do you share your feelings with other people who care about you?

Give Me Time

Action Questions

What internal work do you believe needs to be done in your mind, heart, soul, body, and spirit?

_____
_____
_____
_____
_____
_____
_____
_____
_____
_____
_____
_____
_____
_____
_____
_____
_____
_____
_____
_____
_____
_____
_____
_____
_____

Give Me Time

Action Questions

What boundaries do you have in your life right now? Have you honored these boundaries? Do you need to add or change any boundaries?

Give Me Time

Prayer

Dear Heavenly Father,

Thank You that Your grace is greater than my wounds. I thank You for being Jehovah Rapha, My Healer. Lord, I need emotional healing.

I need You to do a total transformation in my heart, mind, and soul. So, I invite You into the unhealed and broken places within me. Lord, shine Your light in me and reveal to me the areas I need healing in.

Illuminate the things from my past that are causing me continuous cycles of pain and shame. Give me the courage and strength to deal with the things I have been ignoring and teach me how to love myself and others, so that my relationships are healthy and balanced.

Lord, help me to live according to Your will and plans for my life, instead of the plans others have for me.

I ask these things in Your Son Jesus name. Amen

Re-writing A New Story

"Do not cling to events of the past or dwell on what happened long ago. Watch for the new thing I am going to do. It is happening already—you can see it now!"
- Isaiah 43:18-19

━━━ Re-Writing A New Chapter ━━━

Writing A New Story

Rejection and I have a love hate relationship. I hate being rejected with a passion. I'm sure no one likes being rejected, but I hate it! I used to view rejection as my arch enemy.

After being rejected so many times, I felt like rejection was always going to be my fate. So, I decided why even bother dating or hoping for love. I carried that sentiment around with me for years until I gave myself permission to fully go through the nine phases in this book.

Healing from rejection is a choice that requires vulnerability, openness, honesty, and time. Not only is it a choice, it's a journey. For the last four years, I have been on that journey. I have been doing the inner healing work in my heart, mind, body, spirit, and soul. Rejection has stolen some of the best years of my life, but I refuse to let it steal anymore.

One of the first decisions I made when I started this journey was to re-write my story. I had to change the narrative from rejection being my enemy to rejection being my teacher. I believe whenever you keep repeating the same cycles in your life, there is something you are failing to learn. When I looked at my past rejections from that perspective, I began to see real growth and progress in my healing journey.

Instead of despising rejection, I embraced it. I became its student. In my personal time with God, I asked Him what was rejection trying to teach me. What am I failing to learn? These questions, along with intensive prayer and fasting, helped me discover that rejection was trying to teach me how to love, appreciate, and value myself.

Re-Writing A New Chapter

If I would haven't done those three things, I would have keep experiencing rejection in relationships with men because I was trying to make them do something that I had failed to do myself.

As they say, "you are what you attract," and it's true. I kept attracting men who didn't love or value me because I didn't love or value myself. I allowed the lies of the devil to make me believe that since my father had rejected me, I was unworthy of love from men.

So, I held on to relationships with men who showed me time and time again that they didn't appreciate or value me. I believed their crumbs of affection were better than nothing. This negative belief system was one of the many reasons I kept repeating the cycles of rejection.

In retrospection, I picked men who were emotionally unavailable to me because I was emotionally unavailable to myself, and they mirrored that back to me.

Through this journey, I have learned how to love myself unconditionally. I looked at the woman in the mirror and decided she needed to make a change. I spent quality time with God and meditated on scriptures about His eternal love for me, until I was able to give that love to myself.

When I began to love myself, everything about me and everything around me changed. I became more self-confident, and I stopped viewing myself as a victim. Rejection loves to tell you that you're a victim, and the people who reject you are villains. I bought into that false story until God showed me that rejection serves a purpose.

Re-Writing A New Chapter

If Jesus didn't get rejected by the Jews, He would have never made it to the Cross, and if He didn't make it the Cross and die for the sins of the world, then you and I would not have an opportunity to receive eternal life and salvation. Jesus had to be rejected so that He could fulfill His destiny upon this earth. I had to keep getting rejected, so that I could learn to stop rejecting myself. My rejections served a purpose.

Now, I look at all of them in a positive light. I look at them now as necessary experiences that I had to go through in order to learn self-acceptance and self-love. I thank God for everything I have learned on this journey of healing. Healing from rejection hasn't been easy, but it has definitely been worth it. Through releasing my old story, I have been able to re-write a new one, one where I'm the victor and not the victim.

Today, I walk in forgiveness. Today, I walk in freedom. Today, I walk in gratefulness. Today, I walk in wholeness. Today, I walk in peace. Today, I walk in joy. Today, I walk in love. Today, I walk into the newness that God has for me, and I leave the old story of rejection behind. I am stronger, I am wiser, and I am more refined. I am not who rejection says I am. I am who God says I am, and God says that I am healed, and so are you.

Re-Writing A New Chapter

New Day

It's a new season; it's a new day.
I cried my last tears yesterday.
I am looking forward to new beginnings.
No more mourning over past relationship endings.
God has better instore for me, so I left yesterday behind.
Walking forward with a new sense of freedom and peace of mind.
This is my season, this is my hour, this is my time—no more delay.
I rejoice, it's a new day!

Re-Writing A New Chapter

Reflect on when you first started this journey. The road to recovery has not been a straight ride. It has definitely been bumpy at times. You took a couple of detours along the way, but you got back on track. Now, look at yourself. You are growing. You are healing. You are changing for the better. You outlasted the heartbreak and disappointment. Now, turn the page and begin a new chapter.

Re-write the story of your rejection and clear the slate of your past. Speak what you want to see manifested in your life. Speak your future, not your past! Pray daily and pray for the person that rejected you. Pray that God blesses them and releases them into their destiny. Your paths were meant to cross, but only for a season.

At the beginning phases of your healing journey, it was okay for you to put up emotional walls, but now, it's time for you to take those walls down. Don't allow rejection to destroy your future happiness. Take this time now and enjoy life.

Surround yourself with friends and family who remind you that you are valued, loved, accepted, and wanted. Remember, you are accepted into God's beloved family. You are His child. You are loved, and you are appreciated. Don't let one man's rejection of you make you believe or feel otherwise.

The rejection, though painful, taught you the necessary lessons you needed to learn. You have emerged from the rejection with strong insights about who you are and what you want. In each phase of the journey, you pulled back the layers of pain and dissected them.

Re-Writing A New Chapter

The pain, anger, frustration, breakdowns, and, sometimes, failing attempts to grow and progress were necessary and a part of the journey. Everything you felt and experienced was necessary to help you learn the valuable lessons of giving yourself everything the person that rejected you couldn't.

You have learned how to love yourself unconditionally, acknowledge your needs and wants, and become the listening ear you always wanted them to be. The experience of the rejection was essential to helping you become the person you needed to become today.
I cannot guarantee that you will never get rejected again. However, I can promise you that if you do, you will have the tools and experience you need to get through it.

Continue on your path of healing and growth and be open to receiving new love when it comes. Exciting and new opportunities are on the horizon for you. Believe it and receive it. You truly deserve it. Trust and believe that there are more beautiful moments ahead for you.

Re-Writing A New Chapter

New Story

Now, I share my story.
Through me, God will get the glory.
I have been set apart.
I have been given a new heart.
I have been given a fresh start.
I left sadness, bitterness, wrath, and anger behind.
I picked up love, joy, peace, patience, kindness, goodness, faithfulness, gentleness, and self-control when I renewed my mind.
Behold, the former things have passed away, and I have become like new wine.
I now walk in righteousness and purity.
I have put away the sins of my youth and I now live a life of integrity.
For the Master has use of me.
He called me out of my obscurity.
He said, "Amber, share your story.
Your shame, your heartache, and your pain will be used to give Me glory.
There are people you must help, heal, deliver, and restore."
So, no, I am not the same person anymore.
I am moving forward to reach that high mark.
A new journey in ministry, I embark.

Re-Writing A New Chapter

Circumstance Questions

What has rejection taught you?

_____
_____
_____
_____
_____

In what ways are you optimistic about the future?

_____
_____
_____
_____
_____
_____
_____
_____

What are some things you want to see manifested in your life?

_____
_____
_____
_____
_____
_____
_____

Re-Writing A New Chapter
Circumstance Questions

What are some things that you have done lately that you are proud of?

_____
_____
_____
_____
_____
_____
_____
_____
_____
_____

What are your biggest goals before the end of this year? Are you close? What do you need to do to complete these goals?

_____
_____
_____
_____
_____
_____
_____
_____
_____
_____
_____
_____

Re-Writing A New Chapter

Thought Questions

I am looking forward to...

A mantra that I live by...

I want to travel to...

My favorite way to spend the day is

Some new hobbies I would like to try are...

I have a dream to...

Re-Writing A New Chapter
Thought Questions

What do you think your God given purpose is? What are you most passionate about?

List five things you're most grateful for.

Re-Writing A New Chapter
Action Questions

What brings you the most genuine joy and how can you incorporate that joy into your daily life?

_____
_____
_____
_____
_____
_____
_____
_____
_____
_____
_____

What acts of self-care truly make you happy? What self-care activities can you incorporate in your daily life?

_____
_____
_____
_____
_____
_____
_____
_____
_____
_____

Re-Writing A New Chapter

Action Questions

Make a list of positive affirmations and scriptures that you will recite over yourself daily.

_____
_____
_____
_____
_____
_____
_____
_____
_____
_____
_____
_____
_____
_____
_____
_____
_____
_____
_____
_____
_____
_____
_____
_____
_____
_____
_____
_____
_____
_____
_____

Re-Writing A New Chapter

Prayer

Dear Heavenly Father,

Thank You for Your amazing love and grace and for always protecting and guiding me.

Lord, it's time for me to begin a new chapter in my life. As I embrace this new beginning, I ask that You continue to order my steps and fill me with supernatural wisdom, knowledge, and understanding.

Sharpen my discernment so I may be able to recognize relationships and opportunities that are not in Your will for my life. Also, help me to view my past rejections as Your divine redirection and protection.

Now Father, I stand on Your promises that if I continue to seek You with all my heart and soul, You will grant me the desires of my heart (Psalm 37:4) and I will not lack any good thing (Psalm 34:10).

Lord, I desire someone who will love, appreciate, and value me the way You do, and I will not settle for anything less.

Thank You that old things are passing away in this season and all things are becoming new. I decree and declare that gladness and joy is over taking me, and sorrow and sighing is fleeing away.

I ask these things in Your Son Jesus name. Amen

Scriptures To Remember

"My father and mother may abandon me, but the Lord will take care of me." -**Psalm 27:10**

"So we are convinced that every detail of our lives is continually woven together to fit into God's perfect plan of bringing good into our lives, for we are his lovers who have been called to fulfill his designed purpose."-**Romans 8:28**

"The Lord is near to the brokenhearted and saves the crushed in spirit."-**Psalm 34:18**

"He heals the brokenhearted, binding up their wounds." -**Psalm 147:3**

"My health fails; my spirits droop, yet God remains! He is the strength of my heart; he is mine forever!" -**Psalms 73:26**

"To the praise of the glory of his grace, wherein he hath made us accepted in the beloved." -**Ephesians 1:6**

"I have loved you with an everlasting love; therefore I have drawn you with loving devotion." -**Jeremiah 31:3**

"But you are a chosen people, a royal priesthood, a holy nation, God's special possession, that you may declare the praises of him who called you out of darkness into his wonderful light."- **1 Peter 2:9**

About The Author

Amber Nicole Bryant is an author, entrepreneur, spiritual teacher, and founder of She Writes It Ministries, an online Christian ministry dedicated to encouraging, equipping, and empowering people in their daily faith walk with Christ through prophetic writings, prayers, videos, audio messages, and free spiritual resources.

As a master storyteller, Amber uses her unique gift of writing to tell stories that heal and break people free from their spiritual, mental, and emotional bondages. If you are ready to learn, she is ready to teach. Connect with her by visiting and subscribing to her website, www.shewritesit.com.

fb.com/SheIsAWriter   @She_IsAWriter   @She_IsAWriter

www.SheWritesIt.com

Looking For More Spiritual Inspiration?

The Secret Place Prayer Journal

Everything you need can be found in the presence of God and through this journal, you can record your daily encounters with Your Heavenly Father and the revelations you receive from His Word.

This 3-month journal features: Two full pages to journal your daily gratitude to God, bible verses, things on your heart, confession and repentance of sins, revelations from God's Word, and revelations from God's heart.

Early Do I Seek Thee Devotional

Early Do I Seek Thee: 31 Days of Seeking God in the Morning is a Christian Devotional for those ready to take their personal relationship with God to the next level.

The scriptures, devotionals, and affirmations in this book will give you the spiritual insights you need to activate your faith and ignite your love for God in a deeper way. Give God the first few minutes of your morning and watch Him transform your whole day!

Get your copies of these books on Amazon or by visiting www.shewritesit.com

www.ingramcontent.com/pod-product-compliance
Lightning Source LLC
Chambersburg PA
CBHW051542230426
43669CB00015B/2694